COP

WOODS COP

By

John Wasserman

ISBN 978-0-578-68302-7

www.woodscop.org

Cover photo by Denise Mitcheltree

To my wife Denise, for encouraging me to write this book.

Decal used on PA Game Commission Vehicles circa 1975

Introduction

When I began my career with the Pennsylvania Game Commission back in 1975, we were known as district game protectors. Many years later, our title was changed to wildlife conservation officer, and most recently to state game warden. Perhaps you are wondering why I chose the title *Woods Cop* for my book. Well folks, it's a nickname some people use for game wardens while meaning no disrespect. Like when the police are referred to as POPO, a somewhat humorous and inoffensive title. The term POPO originated in California, where bicycle police wore shirts with the insignia PO (police officer) and rode in pairs...POPO. It's a mystery as to where the term Woods Cop originated. Perhaps right here in Penn's Woods.

Back in 1975, our state patrol vehicles had official decals on the doors that depicted the keystone symbol (Pennsylvania's nickname is the Keystone State) along with the inscription *Pennsylvania Game Commission*. The image of a perfectly symmetrical eight-point buck appeared on the keystone.

One day early in my career, after parking my patrol car across from the district judge's office in Renovo, I noticed a small boy standing on the sidewalk near the passenger door. He was no more than seven or eight years old, and staring intently at the official decal on my car. I was wearing civilian clothes that day, a suit and tie, as I was about to present a case before the court. After I exited my car, I heard the young lad call, "Hey mister!" I walked around to the sidewalk and looked down at him. He was dressed in a red flannel shirt with long sleeves rolled up to his elbows. His blue jeans were grass stained on the knees, and his hands were shoved deep in his pockets. He looked straight into my eyes with a very serious expression on his face.

"Something I can help you with?" I asked.

The young lad pointed at the decal and exclaimed, "If you shoot more than you're supposed to, the Woods Cop will get you!"

"You're right, he will, and thanks for the advice," I replied.

The boy smiled back at me, happy that I agreed with him.

"Goodbye mister," he said. Then he turned and walked away, soon rounding a corner and out of sight. I stood there for a moment, grinning ear to ear. It was time for this Woods Cop to get to work. I had a poaching case to prosecute. Something about shooting too many deer, as I recall.

AUTHOR'S NOTE

The incidents recounted in this book are real; however, the stories are based on my memories over a period of years and may differ from the memories of others. I admit to taking some creative liberties with events and to re-creating some of the dialog. I have also given the poachers and their associates fictitious names and have altered their physical descriptions. Any resemblance to actual persons, living or dead, is entirely coincidental.

I'm roaming with the deer tonight.
While poachers search the woods at night
with guns and brilliant beams of light,
a thin green veil will guard this night.
I'm roaming with the deer tonight.
~John Wasserman

X

Prologue

I SERVED AS A PENNSYLVANIA state game warden for 34 years including a two-year stint as a deputy. My patrol district consisted of a 450 square mile chunk of the most rugged and isolated terrain in the state. It is 95 percent forested with narrow valleys and steep side-hills and doesn't contain a single farm. The Clinton County district was centered within several contiguous tracts of state forest land in northcentral Pennsylvania comprising about 1.5 million acres, and represents one of the largest sections of wild country in the eastern United States. Nearby, is the Allegheny National Forest, which covers an additional half million acres of land.

There are very few paved roads in northern Clinton County, most are dirt or gravel and not maintained during winter. The streams are called runs; they are narrow, steep, fast-moving bodies of cold, crystal clear water teeming with native brook trout. Wildlife abounds here, and besides a large population of deer and bear, there are elk, bobcats, fishers, otters, ravens, eagles and other animals found in remote wild areas.

In May of 2006, *National Geographic Adventure* magazine described the wildness of northcentral Pennsylvania as "on par with Brazil's Pantanal and China's Gobi as one of the last untarnished tracts on earth." Considered one of the most sparsely populated locations in the eastern U.S., this area is featured in the book *The Last Empty Places* by world traveler and author Peter Stark.

About 3,000 people resided in the six townships that comprised my patrol district in northern Clinton County. The vast majority of the population was located in and around the adjoining river towns of Renovo, Farwell, and North Bend.

Outside of these three communities are the woods, often referred to as the "big woods," which served as my patrol district. There is only one traffic light in more than 1,000 square miles, and it has long since served its purpose from back in the day when Renovo was a booming railroad town. Now it remains at the intersection of the Elk Scenic Drive and the Bucktail Trail, serving mostly as a nuisance where a stop sign would suffice.

Surrounded by the steep side-hills of the Appalachian Plateau, Renovo is a mile-long slice of a town squeezed between an extensive line of railroad tracks and the West Branch of the Susquehanna River. The town was constructed back in the mid-1800s by the Philadelphia & Erie Railroad because it was halfway between those two cities and served as a stopover point for trains traveling between them. Over the next 100 years the town grew, and the railroad company gradually built shops to manufacture and repair railroad cars.

Berwick Forge & Fabricating, a railroad freight car manufacturer with a workforce of hundreds, was the biggest employer in northern Clinton County when I was assigned to this area in 1976. I can vividly remember the first time I observed workers leaving the plant at the end of their shift. Tired and soiled, they crossed twelve lines of railroad using a steel footbridge twenty feet high that stretched from the factory to Erie Avenue.

Renovo was a very unusual town in those days. It seemed as if I had entered a time warp and was transported back to the 1950s. The Pennsylvania Railroad YMCA was a great example of this. Built in 1913, it was located in a large four story brick building at the end of town and served the local people well. It contained a 65,000-gallon indoor swimming pool, a large gymnasium, a four-lane bowling alley, a restaurant, and was open 24 hours every day. However, if you wanted to bowl, you needed to hire a pin setter for each lane. Teenagers looking for a way to earn a little money were happy to take the job. There was also lodging available, as the building contained several floors of rooms, although many were set aside for the railroaders. The hotel was always booked full during hunting season.

The Bucktail Trail Scenic Byway from Hyner to North Bend.

All police calls went to the YMCA, as the base radio for the Renovo Police Department was located there. Whoever was working the cash register also took police calls for the officer on duty. If no one was on duty, the state police would be called at a substation some 30 miles away.

During autumn of 1982, the A&P supermarket closed leaving dozens out of a job. Berwick Forge & Fabricating pulled out of town and hundreds were laid off. Conrail stopped using Renovo to change train crews. The YMCA Restaurant and Hotel, where Conrail crews stayed, and the heart of the town's recreational activity, closed. The Piper Aircraft plant closed its doors and more than 100 workers lost their jobs. Then only a few days later, a fire completely leveled three other major businesses, and unemployment in Renovo reached a staggering 85 percent. Poaching was rampant, and it was a very grim and challenging time to be a state game warden here.

To those devoid of imagination, a blank place on the map is a useless waste; to others, the most valuable part.
~Aldo Leopold, *A Sand County Almanac*

Winter Kill

In the beginning of my career, I had two deputies: Gerald Conahan and "Ranger." I met Gerald when I first arrived here in 1976, and we soon became good friends. Gerald was a deputy waterways patrolman (fish warden) at the time, and we worked together as often as possible. Two years later our mutual friend and fellow officer Lloyd Wilson died. Lloyd had been the Clinton County district waterways patrolman for many years up until his death, and Gerald was his deputy. It was soon after Lloyd died that Gerald came on board with me as a deputy game warden. He was a terrific storyteller, and always had a supply of amusing encounters with other people.

On September 19, 1981, Gerald and I started work together at about 8 PM. It was a quiet night and his tall tales and clever jokes kept us awake, laughing often, until 4 AM when we decided to pack it in. I dropped Gerald off at his home and then went to my house for some shuteye. I had just fallen asleep when my telephone rang, jarring me back to consciousness. Renovo Police Officer Clark Cannon was on the other end of the line.

"John, sorry to wake you," he said. He paused for a moment before continuing. "I'm afraid I have some bad news; Gerald Conahan passed away early this morning."

I was stunned! He suffered a massive heart attack right after he walked into the house. Gerald was only 44 years old, and his death was completely unexpected. I had Gerald's badge sealed in Lucite (a solid transparent plastic) and presented it to his youngest son. Almost 40 years have passed, and I miss him to this very day.

It was on a cold mid-January day back in 1978 when Deputy Conahan watched a young lad named Billy Bandito shoot at a turkey. Gerald just happened to be looking out his living room window while the teenager was aiming his rifle. The season had long been over, but Billy didn't seem to care much about that. He wasn't concerned about being in Deputy Conahan's Safety Zone either. Legally, a Safety Zone is that distance within 150 yards of a home, and is closed to hunting without permission of the occupant. Billy saw the turkey sitting on the limb of a tree and couldn't resist the temptation to shoot it.

Boom! The rifle recoiled, and smoke puffed out of the barrel. Gerald didn't realize it at the time, but the boy actually missed the turkey and inadvertently shot the limb right out from under the bewildered bird. When the turkey hit the snow, it sank so deep that it could barely flap its wings. Weak from lack of food, the bird grew tired quickly as it struggled in the bottomless white powder. A stronger bird might have lifted off, but this one was trapped.

Gerald quickly put on his boots and waded through nearly three feet of snow toward the hunter. Billy was standing near the downed bird by then, and because Gerald knew his family, he sent him home and went back inside for a blanket to cover the "wounded" turkey. Once it's head was covered it quickly calmed down, and Gerald, still thinking the bird was wounded, took the turkey inside, put it on the floor in his living room, and walked into the kitchen to call me. Then, while he was explaining what had happened, I suddenly heard a lot of commotion in the background. Gerald's wife was screaming while their kids were laughing hysterically. The turkey, it turned out, had made a quick and complete recovery and began flying around Gerald's living room. It was on a collision course with everything, and I don't think there was a lamp left standing by the time Gerald subdued the frantic bird!

By then, it was obvious that the turkey wasn't wounded after all, and it was promptly released. Once things settled down in the house, Gerald figured he had better backtrack Billy to see what other kind of trouble he may have gotten into. This kid was the type who would shoot an animal just for target practice, as was the case in this instance. His mom wouldn't let him bring anything into the house that had been taken illegally, so whatever he killed usually remained where it dropped. Gerald had gone only a couple hundred yards into the woods when he saw a pair of turkey legs protruding out of the snow. The same footprints clearly indicated that this bird had been designated as another one of Billy's living targets.

Gerald eventually caught up to him, and he was fined for each of the two turkeys and had his hunting privileges revoked for several years. It would have been nice if Billy had learned a lesson, but unfortunately, he didn't.

Nine years later, Billy was with two of his buddies when they shot a deer shortly after leaving a bar near the village of Cross Fork in Potter County. It was during daylight hours, and fortunately, I had a witness.

The three men were dragging the deer out of the woods toward the road when a camp owner in the area stopped his car behind Billy's pickup truck, which was "parked" in the middle of the road with the doors open and the engine running. With that, the three poachers immediately let go of the deer and ran to the truck while shielding their faces with their hands. What they didn't realize is that the witness already saw enough to identify them. Seems he had shared a friendly drink or two with the men from time to time at that same bar in Cross Fork. But because he was driving his brother's car and wearing a hat and sunglasses, they didn't recognize him as they scrambled into Billy's pickup and headed back to Renovo.

The witness was very angry about what he saw, and immediately drove to a phone booth to call me. I met with him in Cross Fork later that afternoon and followed him to the scene. I found a .22 caliber shell casing on the roadway and put it in my pocket. From there, I could see the deer lying in the brush at the woods' edge. As we approached, I noticed a slight movement from its hind leg. Billy and his accomplices were in such a hurry to load the illegal deer into their truck and get it out of sight, I don't think they cared that it was still alive. It couldn't put up a fight, as the bullet had pierced its spine, rendering it helpless. I dispatched the deer, field dressed it, and gave it to a needy family living nearby.

People don't think straight when they've been drinking heavily. Shooting a deer from a state roadway isn't very smart, even in this remote part of the state where the odds of being seen were extremely low. But it was senseless to take the risk. There were plenty of deer in the area, with several isolated forestry roads they could have used to kill a deer on their way back to town.

Most closed-season deer kills in these parts happen under the cover of darkness while using a spotlight and a .22 caliber rifle. Used at night, deep in the woods while traveling dirt and gravel forest roads, it is the method of choice for most poachers. But this was a spur-of-the-moment decision for Billy. The deer was standing broadside only 50 yards from the road, and he couldn't resist killing it. If Billy had shut his engine off before running into the woods for the deer, he would have heard my witnesses' car as it came up the road behind him. But the loud rumble of his rusty old Ford pickup, with no muffler, made it impossible to hear any approaching vehicles.

Had they been able to load the deer into Billy's truck, their intent was to take it to a remote spot along Kettle Creek, remove the backstraps and hindquarters, and leave the remainder back in the woods for the buzzards to eat. Most poachers despise wasting part of any kill, illegal or otherwise. I've had a few provide me with information about other poachers who failed to live up to this "outlaw standard practice." Here the infamous Clinton County poacher called Coyotee Boy comes to mind. But I'll get to him later.

Ranger and I cornered all three poachers in town later that evening. Billy was drunk when we stopped his pickup, and he wasn't feeling very cooperative. Neither he nor his buddies,

Tom and Rick, were going to admit to anything. And although we couldn't detain the men any longer after questioning them, I wasn't about to let Billy drive anywhere in his present condition, so I radioed the Renovo Police and turned him over to officers Cannon and Fantaskey (it would be another ten years until the law was amended allowing state game wardens to enforce DUI infractions).

Billy Bandito was later convicted for drunk driving, and thanks to my witness, all three poachers were also found guilty of killing a deer in closed season. Each of them paid a $400 fine plus whatever their attorney charged them for his time during the three-hour-long hearing before the district judge in Renovo. In addition, Billy, Tom and Rick each had their hunting and trapping privileges revoked for three years.

Two years later, we caught Rick doing it all over again. He was convicted, fined, and had an additional three years tacked on to his revocation. For some, it seems poaching is a way of life.

The winter of 1977-78 had been a disaster for wild turkeys, and the winter of 1981-82 proved to be just as deadly. But this time it was the deer herd that suffered. A freak ice storm in January, 1982 caused untold suffering to the deer herd in northern Clinton County. The rugged mountains here were glazed with a solid sheet of ice that remained for weeks. Steep hillsides became slippery frozen ramps that sent hundreds of deer sprawling helplessly downhill through an obstacle course of timber, all too often to a grisly demise.

It began as a sleet storm one cold, blustery Friday night. When it was over, eight inches of granular ice covered the ground. I had never seen anything like it before. Huge piles of sleet were formed at the bottoms of mountainous "cuts" that ran down rocky side-hills along local roadways. These cuts had been gouged out by natural water runoff over the course of eons and acted as a funnel, sending tons of sleet to the highways wherever they were found. Giant mounds of ice pellets reached heights of 60 to 70 feet in some areas along the Bucktail Trail (State Route 120), completely shutting down the highway. Along one stretch, there was a mammoth pile of sleet that reached somewhere between 100 and 150 feet high!

In addition to state highway department equipment used to haul the sleet away, there were other larger pieces of equipment utilized to remove the ice pellets. A local coal company hired out a big surface mine wheel loader with a 60-ton bucket payload, and a construction company out of Lock Haven put two large loaders to work.

The problem for the deer began when we got a brief warm spell along with some light rain that melted the surface of the sleet-covering followed by a hard and prolonged freeze, which turned the partially melted sleet into solid ice. The icy crust was hard enough to support the weight of a human, and in some areas you could drive a car over it without breaking through. Fawns had the worst problem because they were too light to get any kind of foothold. The deer would lose their footing and fall spread-eagle on top of the ice, then slide down the steep side-hills, slamming into trees, rocks and logs along the way until finally coming to rest along a road or in a streambed. In many instances, their front legs would spread apart until they became dislocated at the shoulder joints, their pelvic bones splitting as well, which left them totally helpless with all four legs extending straight out from their sides. It was a pitiful sight to say the least, and I spent much of my time that winter putting those hapless creatures out of their misery.

The author with some deer collected from the Kettle Creek Valley in 1982

I remember one incident when I watched a deer slide two hundred yards down a steep, frozen slope, hit a highway guardrail and then continue to slide down another embankment onto the ice-covered Susquehanna River. The deer tried to walk across the ice but could go only a short distance before falling down. After three hours, the deer finally made it to the other side, only to find the bank too steep and icy to climb. Its fate was uncertain, and there was no way for me to rescue it. The river ice was thin, and the deer almost broke through while crossing. Sometimes I found deer standing in streams because the banks were too steep and icy for them to walk out of the water. I really felt helpless then, because all I could do was hope for a quick warm spell.

Snow grooming machine used to get deep into impassable forestry roads.

Most roads were inaccessible by anything other than snowmobiles, so I could only recover a small percentage of the crippled deer. However, I was able to get to some hard-to-reach areas with the use of a Bureau of Forestry snow-grooming machine. Unfortunately, the snow machine would startle some deer and cause them to try running up hill, only to lose footing on the icy crust and slide back down into a tree or boulder. I quickly abandoned this method of deer recovery and assessment of the situation deep in the woods.

Many of the whitetails would lie for days, dying slow deaths. It was very difficult to do any walking in the woods and going uphill or down was nearly impossible. On occasion, however, I got a report of a crippled deer that some surefooted local ridge runner would find, and I'd have him guide me to it so that it could be humanely dispatched.

After three weeks, we finally got a break in the weather, and things began to improve. I personally removed or accounted for a total of 107 deer, and approximately 80 percent of those were fawns. One can only speculate as to what the total loss was, but I estimated a loss of thousands just in my 450 square mile patrol district.

Justice is the constant and perpetual wish to render to everyone his due.

~Emperor Justinian, *Institutione*

The Cross Fork Commando

MIKEY SLAPPED ME ACROSS THE right side of my face and shouted, "*You're weak!*" I could feel a storm brewing inside me as I turned away to face a crowd of more than 100 athletes and spectators. It was spring, circa 1980, and I was competing in powerlifting at the Ontario Police Olympics in Ottawa Canada.

I looked down at the floor and stared at a barbell loaded with 650 pounds of steel weights. Mikey was my training partner, and he did exactly what was needed to snap me out of my passive mental state. This would be my second attempt to make the lift. Maybe I could do it this time. It would be a new personal record for the deadlift, and might even earn a gold medal in my weight class. I walked over to the barbell and stood briefly with my feet midway under the bar before bending over to grasp it in a shoulder-width grip. Then I bent my knees, took a deep breath and pulled with all my might, but the 1/3-ton of dead weight came only a few inches off the floor before I was forced to set it back down. Disheartened, I turned and walked slowly back to the staging area.

Mikey was standing there waiting for me. He grabbed me by the shoulders, looked me in the eye and assured me I would do it on my next attempt. But I had my doubts. I couldn't get it off the floor on my first try, and my second effort wasn't much better. Because I'd have to wait for my competitors to finish their turns before my third and final attempt, I sat down on a nearby wall bench and tried to refocus my thoughts. I had been training for several months for this event, and I wanted to get away from it mentally to relieve some of the stress I was feeling. I leaned back against the wall, closed my eyes, and mused upon my early days as a state game warden…

February is a relatively quiet month in northern Clinton County. The hunting seasons have ended, and most of the state forest roads are virtually shut down by ice and snow, as these dirt and gravel lanes are not maintained in winter. I could finally start to live a more normal lifestyle that included a workweek with less evening hours. It was also the time when I could begin training for both the Pennsylvania Police Olympics and Ontario Police Olympics held each spring.

Up until the early 1980s, February always marked the start of the beaver trapping season, usually beginning in the middle of the month and ending in mid-March. I spent a good deal of my time hiking along frozen beaver ponds scattered sporadically within those icy streams containing suitable habitat. Trappers would be on their best behavior this time of year because weather conditions made their trap sets difficult to conceal from the local game warden. I remember one individual, however, who didn't care about the rules. He epitomized the scurrilous villain trapper so often falsely portrayed in both movies and literature. He was known locally as the Cross Fork Commando. I knew him as Ziggy Badd, and had a number of confrontations with him over the years.

When I arrived in this remote district in the mid-1970s, Ziggy had already established himself as an outlaw to be reckoned with. He had a reputation for incomparable stealth in the woods. It was said that Ziggy hunted every day, but he was rarely seen by other hunters. Occasionally, he would appear from the shadowed woodlands dressed in full camouflage, painted face, rifle in hand, and then just as quickly vanish in thick underbrush or laurel. The Commando always wore camouflage, even when he wasn't hunting and trapping. He used the US Army "leaf pattern" camo officially known as ERDL, worn by soldiers during the Vietnam War. Ziggy had shoulder-length brown hair with a mustache and full beard neatly cropped. He stood six feet tall with a lean muscular build, high cheekbones and bright (some would say eerily intense) green eyes, making him widely recognizable. It was the rare color of his eyes that set him apart, possessed by less than two percent of the world population.

I remember an elderly long-time hunter from Cross Fork who told me about the one and only time he saw Ziggy in the woods. The hunter was up in a portable treestand and dressed in full camo. Other than a downy woodpecker quietly pecking away at a tree, there was a dead calm. Suddenly he spotted Ziggy directly under his treestand looking up at him. He was carrying a bow, and had a dead yearling deer over his shoulders. Ziggy winked and slowly walked away without making a sound. "There's no way that's possible!" the hunter told me. "Nobody can sneak up on me like that without me hearing them coming!"

I had only been in my new district for a few weeks when I first met the Commando. I was fishing along Kettle Creek on a warm summer evening when I heard a shot from up the valley. I quickly reeled in my line, jumped into the car, and headed in that direction. As I approached some distant fields, I spotted an old Jeep, painted military green, stopped in the middle of the road. I pulled over before being completely exposed and watched with my binoculars. I heard the horn blow once, and I could see the driver turning his head left and right scanning the fields on both sides of the road. Soon the car started to move forward, and I continued watching until it was out of sight. I suspected the driver had fired the shot I heard before, most likely at a groundhog, so I returned to the area in my patrol car the following day and positioned myself on a hill with a good view of the field.

After about two hours, the same Jeep appeared. Ever so slowly, it cruised down an old road that ran adjacent to the field I was watching. It wasn't too long before it came to an abrupt stop in the middle of the road. A rifle barrel suddenly appeared from a side window and a shot was fired into the field. I rushed to the scene in my patrol car and pulled up behind the Jeep. It hadn't moved since the shot was fired, and it was only then that I realized four people were crammed into it. The radio was blasting away so loud that they didn't realize I was behind them as I exited my vehicle and walked to the back of Jeep. The rear plastic window was missing, so I reached in and pulled the rifle out from between two surprised occupants while announcing my presence.

I told the driver to step out of the car and ordered the rest of the men to remain inside. Suddenly I realized I was face to face with the Cross Fork Commando! He didn't say anything, just stared at me, never blinked. I could feel something primitive, wild, about his presence, but I shook it off and told myself he was just a man, not some legendary character who stalked the local woodlands in ghostly silence. I told Ziggy Badd he was in violation of the Pennsylvania Game Law for hunting from a motor vehicle.

"You didn't have to work too hard for this one," he said. "But you would never have caught me if I'd stayed in the woods."

"Think so?" I said, still waiting for him to blink just once. But Ziggy didn't answer; he just stood there eyeing me with a cold stare. He paid his fine in cash right on the spot (in those days, game wardens often collected fines in cash and issued a field receipt to the violator), and it was obvious from our first meeting that Ziggy and I were not going to get along. What wasn't so obvious was the short period of time before I would run into him again.

It was the 1977 beaver trapping season that brought us together once more. I was checking a beaver dam on a cold gray February afternoon near the village of Cross Fork when I came upon two steel-jawed foothold traps. The law required that traps must be at least 25 feet from a beaver dam or lodge, and these traps were only 15 feet away. I checked the nametags on each of them and discovered they belonged to Ziggy Badd, so I sprung both traps and put a note between the jaws of one explaining why they were unlawfully set. Most people are thankful when they get a warning rather than a fine, but not Ziggy. I found out later that he was angry because I "messed with his traps," and heard that he'd been in a local bar bragging how he was going to handle me the next time we met. Although I figured it was nothing more than barroom bravado, I intended to be more cautious with him in the future.

After a couple weeks passed, I returned to the beaver dam where I had sprung Ziggy's traps. There was fresh beaver activity, but for some reason the Commando didn't have any traps set. This wasn't like Ziggy, I thought. After careful scrutiny, I noticed a small channel of water spilling over the dam. It appeared to be man-made and was just wide enough to conceal a foothold trap. I had a hunch that someone was trying to be tricky, so I decided to return late that night.

I arrived back at the dam shortly after ten o'clock. Sure enough, there was an untagged size 4 Victor double long spring trap set in the channel and wired to a nearby sapling. I sprung the trap to prevent a beaver from being captured and found a secluded spot to hide my state vehicle. The beaver pond ran parallel to Kettle Creek Road, which is paved and follows the creek to its confluence with the West Branch of the Susquehanna River.

I climbed partway up a steep hillside adjacent to the roadway and situated myself behind some beech trees where I could observe the dam. It was a very cold night with temperatures in the mid-twenties and a bright full moon, which made visibility good. I was prepared to stay all night if necessary, so I brought along a heavy wool blanket and thermos of coffee to help keep me reasonably warm. At this point, I wasn't sure who the trapper was, but I had a very strong hunch that Ziggy and I were about to meet again.

Hours passed with only a half-dozen cars traveling by my position. By 2:00 AM, it was very cold and extremely quiet. I began to doze off when a sudden loud and sharp sound, like the crack of a whip, brought me to my senses. I jumped up and peered into the darkness. There was still plenty of moonlight, and I was only 50 yards from the pond, but I couldn't see a thing. Then I heard it again, but this time I knew what it was. I was wide awake by now and able to detect a splashing sound at the same instant. It was the telltale sound that a beaver makes when it slaps its flat tail on the surface of the water in an effort to quickly submerge. With a sigh of relief, I sat back down and poured a hot cup of black coffee.

Another hour passed and not a single vehicle had gone by. Mr. Beaver was keeping me awake with his occasional power dives, but it was starting to get very cold, and as the temperature dropped, it became increasingly difficult to stay warm.

Suddenly the low rumble of a distant motor vehicle made me forget all about the stinging cold air. As the vehicle got closer, it was obvious that it had no muffler and was traveling at an excessive rate of speed. The noise continued to grow louder, with the blare of its powerful engine vibrating off the frozen side-hills and echoing up the narrow valley. I knew the Commando had wrecked his Jeep and was driving an old beat-up Chevy with no muffler, and suspected it might be him.

When the car was within 100 feet of the beaver dam, the driver slammed on the brakes sending the car skidding sideways. It came screeching to a halt in the middle of the road, directly across from the beaver dam.

It was Ziggy Badd. Ziggy got out of the car and headed for the dam while I cautiously began working my way down the hillside. I was concerned that my hands and knees were still stiff from sitting for so long in the cold night air. There was a stinging sensation in my fingertips as I rubbed my hands together, desperately trying to be fully prepared for the unknown. I finally reached the road and quietly waited at the woods' edge across from Ziggy's car while he pulled up his trap.

Soon I could see a shadowy figure in the moonlight coming my way from the dam. It was so quiet, I could hear the jingling of the trap chain as he carried it along, but the Commando's footfall was silent. It was a little unnerving. Zero dark thirty in the middle of nowhere and about to face a ghost.

As he placed his trap in the trunk of his car, I stepped out from the woods in full uniform and shoved him against the fender for a pat-down search. Ziggy was unarmed and offered no resistance. I could sense that he was angry with himself for falling into the trap I had set for him. Then he surprised me by telling me that he had suspected something wasn't right when he noticed that the trap was sprung, but hadn't been moved.

"The next time you do this," he said, "toss the trap into the water so it looks like something got caught and pulled out of it!" Ziggy's eyes narrowed, his face a mask of contempt. "I should've known better," he grumbled. "I'll bet I even know where you hid your car." Then he pointed to the precise location where I had parked it. "You'll never catch me again!" he declared. "I won't mess up next time."

Ziggy paid his fine a few days later, and his hunting and trapping privileges were revoked for the following hunting license year. It was during that year, on a cold, blustery night, that Ziggy called me on the phone. A deer had been hit by a car in front of his home and he wanted a permit for it. I was surprised that he called because things like permits didn't normally concern Ziggy. I told him that I was going to be out his way later and wanted to examine the deer before issuing any permit.

In those days, every state game warden (called game protectors) had their name, patrol district and home phone number printed in the Game Commission's Hunting and Trapping Digest. And every hunter in the state received a copy of the digest with their respective licenses. In addition, all of us had our phone numbers listed in the local phone book. There were no dispatchers to handle calls; we were expected to available 24/7, and there was no such thing as overtime pay. But I didn't care, it was a way of life for me, and I enjoyed it. Except for the calls at two o'clock in the morning!

I arrived at Ziggy's home later that night and could see the deer hanging from a tree with the headlights of his car shining on the carcass. Ziggy was deliriously drunk, skinning and quartering the deer purely by instinct. Despite the cold, rainy 45-degree weather, he was clad only in a tattered pair of jeans, a T-shirt and bare feet as he cut away at the carcass. This guy can't be human, I thought. When I got out of my car and approached him, he suddenly whipped around facing me. Ziggy's hands were covered with blood, his heavy knife pointed ominously in my direction. Just as quickly, with a laugh, he spun around and slammed the knife into the deer's ribcage. *Thwack!*

"For a second there, I thought I'd have to shoot you," I said with a taut grin. With that remark, Ziggy laughed again. Then he cocked his chin at the moon and let out a long, wolf-like howl. He always was a hard man to understand.

I carefully examined the deer, determined it had been hit by a motor vehicle, and gave him his permit. As I backed my patrol car out of his driveway, Ziggy went to work on the deer. I wondered if he realized he was standing on its entrails as he carved away on the carcass. Perhaps he didn't care.

The following year, Ziggy's revocation ended and he could legally hunt and trap. While I didn't see him during the hunting season, our paths crossed again during beaver season. I received a tip that he was running more than the maximum limit of ten traps. I also knew from past information that he would take more than the legal limit of three beavers during a single season. There weren't many beavers in my district, and I knew where all the dams were located, so I carefully checked each of these locations and was able to locate eight of Ziggy's traps. Each morning, I left my headquarters (my home) before daybreak to check Ziggy's trapline before he did. This was the only way I could determine whether or not he was taking over the limit.

On the second day of the season, he caught a beaver in a bodygripping trap set in an underwater bank den. I photographed it and noted the date, time and location. Several days later, he had another one in a foothold trap, and it was still alive. Before I could count that one as being legally "taken" I had to be able to verify he killed it. I drove up a steep state forest road to an area on the facing mountain where I could conceal my vehicle and watch the beaver with binoculars. After nearly three hours, Ziggy still hadn't arrived to check his trap, and I was getting impatient.

About that time, a second trapper showed up at the beaver pond, as he too had some traps set at that location. The trapper wasn't a local, so I figured the odds were favorable that he didn't know Ziggy. I took a chance and drove down to meet him. He turned out to be very friendly and cooperative. Just as I had figured, he didn't know Ziggy, but he had heard of him. I gave the trapper directions to his home and asked him to go over and tell Ziggy there was a beaver in one of his traps. Then I went back up to my lookout post and waited. Within minutes, the Commando showed up. He opened the door of his car and out jumped a small brown and white dog, followed by the man himself. Ziggy walked up to the beaver, shot it in the head and put the carcass in the trunk of his car. I made another entry in my notebook.

A cold front moved in that night bringing snow, and everything froze up solid. This made beaver trapping much more difficult. Days went by and Ziggy wasn't catching anything. I still knew where eight of his traps were set, so I took a ride up Cross Fork Creek Road in Potter County on a hunch that I might find more. After traveling a couple miles, I rounded a curve and spotted his car in the middle of the road a hundred yards ahead. Ziggy was out of the vehicle putting chains on his rear tires and didn't see me, so I quickly backed up, turned around and headed back to Clinton County.

I returned later that night. It was cold and dark as I slowly cruised along the snow-covered road where I spotted Ziggy earlier. After traveling a few miles, I saw where a car had pulled over, so I got out to take a look. There were footprints headed down an embankment toward the creek with the same tread pattern as Ziggy's boots, and they were accompanied by the tracks of a medium size dog.

I followed the footprints down the steep bank and along the creek, searching for beaver traps. After traveling a half mile, I came upon two of Ziggy's traps: a Number 3 double long spring and a 330 Conibear. The Conibear was a 10" x 10" body-gripping trap, and by law had to be set completely under water. This requirement greatly reduced the possibility that something other than a beaver would be caught by mistake. These traps are unforgiving, and meant almost certain death to any creature passing through the jaws. Ziggy had it set in only a half-inch of water, a clear and flagrant violation of the Game Law. He was so sure he wouldn't be caught that he left his nametag on the trap! I pulled up the Conibear and continued to look for more traps, but didn't find any.

When I contacted Ziggy the next day, he denied setting any traps along Cross Fork Creek.

"Ain't been up there for days," he snorted.

"I discovered two of your traps set there yesterday," I said. "Are you telling me you're not checking them every 36 hours as required by law?"

"Somebody stole some of my traps!" he insisted. "I told you I ain't been there!"

"You had a 330 Conibear illegally set above the waterline," I said. "The trap has your nametag on it."

"Then you better do your job and find out who took my trap and set it there!"

When I told Ziggy I watched him putting chains on his car the day before, he got angry. He told me he wanted his trap back and that I'd better stop harassing him.

"I'm not harassing you; I'm arresting you," I said.

This time Ziggy decided he wanted a hearing on the matter. He had an attorney represent him before District Justice Katherine Flynn in Galeton. Galeton is a small town located along Pine Creek in Potter County, population about 1,100. I presented my case before the court, knowing it would be difficult to prove. However, I kept meticulous notes during my investigation, and provided my testimony in great detail. His attorney argued that I couldn't prove Ziggy set the trap because I didn't actually *see* him do it. But District Justice Flynn believed I had presented strong circumstantial evidence and found him guilty as charged. Ziggy later appealed his conviction to the Potter County Court of Common Pleas and was once again found guilty of the violation. The Commando had his hunting and trapping privileges revoked for the following year.

Years have passed since then, and Ziggy and I still cross paths once in a while. We are on speaking terms now, probably because he gave up beaver trapping. He's much older today, but still legendary to the people who know him as the Cross Fork Commando.

Physical fitness and law enforcement go hand in hand due to the ever-present risk of a physical confrontation. Many state game wardens are involved with a physical fitness program of some sort, and some compete in a variety of sports that require an intensive training schedule. My identical twin brother, Bill, a retired Pennsylvania state game warden in Wyoming County, inspired me to begin weightlifting many years ago. He is a former national bodybuilding champion, and holds a 3rd degree black belt in Karate. My sport of choice was powerlifting, and in February, I would increase my workouts and begin serious training for upcoming competitions. Powerlifting consists of three lifts: the squat, bench press, and deadlift, in that order. In a competition, a lifter gets three attempts for each category, with the goal of reaching your maximum poundage during one of those attempts. I would go for the maximum on my first attempt, knowing if I failed, there would be two more opportunities. However, there is the risk of failing all three attempts, which would eliminate you from the competition. Powerlifters compete in bodyweight classes. Whoever has the highest combined total pounds lifted from their best squat, bench press, and deadlift is the winner of that weight class. My body weight would range between 210-215 pounds at 6 feet tall, so I would compete in 220-pound weight class.

There are strict rules on how each lift is performed: For the bench press, the lifter must lie on his back with shoulders and buttocks in contact with the flat bench surface before lifting the barbell off an upright rack positioned overhead. Next you must lower it to your chest, holding it there for the referee's command to press (this is when seconds feel more like minutes). On the command, you press your arms upright until the elbows are locked and hold for another brief pause until the referee gives the command to rack it (place it back on the uprights). Each lifter will have someone "spotting" for them. For the bench press, this could be someone standing behind the lifter's head, or it could be two people, with a person standing on each side of the barbell. You must not lift your buttocks or your head off the bench during the attempt, and your feet must remain firmly planted on the floor. There are three official referees to score each event.

For the squat, the loaded barbell is lifted off power rack supports by ducking under the bar and positioning your shoulders up and against it, knees slightly bent. Next, you must push up with your legs to free the barbell from the supports, and step back. Then, on command by the referee, you squat downward until the top surface of your legs at the hip joint are just below your knees (at this point, your legs are parallel with the floor). From here, you must be able to stand up straight and hold for the command to rack the weight.

The deadlift is the third and final lift. It is by far the hardest, even though it has the least rules. You have one minute to walk up to the loaded barbell and lift it off the ground, stand straight up, and pause with shoulders back and knees locked. Once you have paused in this position, the command will be given to set the barbell back down while holding on with both hands until it touches the floor on each end. This lift is as much mental as it is physical.

*S*nap out of it, you're next!" shouted Mikey. "What were you thinking about?"

I quickly broke out of my daze. "The Commando," I said.

"Well you better start thinking about lifting that barbell because they just called you to the floor!"

"Ok, I got this," I said as I bit down hard on my mouth guard. But I knew I wasn't prepared mentally. There was no adrenalin surge like what I had earlier with my 400-pound bench press or my 550-pound squat. Each of those lifts could have crushed me (if not for the spotters), so there was that rush, or adrenalin high that helped me push the weight up. But not with the deadlift; the barbell just sat there, motionless, daring me to lift 650 pounds of cold steel off the ground.

Suddenly, Mikey tucked his chin and grabbed the back of my head with both hands, pulling the top of my forehead against his. It was like a slow-motion head butt, and I didn't expect it. This was not part of our training protocol. It hurt!

Mikey's eyes bored into mine. "I was gonna wait until after the competition to tell you this…"

"Tell me what?" I cut in.

"People are talking, complaining."

"About what?"

"Coyotee Boy has been bragging that you never caught him and never will. People in town want him stopped and they've been saying you're afraid of him."

"You should've told me about this, Mike!" I shouted. Mikey had lit a fuse and it was about to explode. I spun around, my eyes riveted on the barbell. On my second attempt, I felt a storm brewing inside me, but this time I felt pure rage.

I tightened my weightlifting belt, chalked my palms, and walked over to the barbell. I stood with my feet midway under the bar, pausing only for a second before bending over and grabbing the bar with a shoulder-width grip. I bent my knees until my shins touched the bar, then slowly lifted my chest while straightening my lower back. I took a deep breath and paused, looking straight ahead without focusing on the crowd of spectators. My body trembled as I pulled with every ounce of strength. I could feel the bar brush against my shins, then my knees and finally my lower thighs. I locked my hips and knees, pulled my shoulders back and made eye contact with the head referee. It seemed like an eternity before he finally signaled me to lower the weight.

John Wasserman with gold medals at the Ontario Police Olympics

I did it! I turned away and walked proudly back to Mikey. He was smiling ear-to-ear as he raised his right hand. We slapped palms and a cloud of chalk dust filled the air. I knew deep down inside that he made up the story about Coyotee Boy. But in a strange sort of way, I wanted to believe him, because I probably couldn't have made the lift otherwise.

"Mikey, that was pretty clever," I said. "You had me for a moment with the story about Coyotee Boy."

"Yeah, but part of it is true, John. People do want him stopped." Mikey was dead serious, and it did sting a little.

"I know it Mikey; his day is coming, and it's just a matter of time."

The powerlifting meet would be over soon. We were anxious for the results, but winners wouldn't be announced until all competitors had completed their lifts. I started thinking about Coyotee Boy and how often people would complain to me about him poaching deer, but it was always secondhand information or after-the-fact. And when I did have an eyewitness, they wouldn't testify in court. There was never enough to get a search warrant, and Coyotee Boy would never admit to anything when questioned. I was deep in thought when the head judge announced the winners for the 220-pound bodyweight class. I won the powerlifting competition for my weight class, and the Champion of Champions gold medal for the heaviest total pounds lifted in excess of body weight, surpassing all lifters regardless of weight class.

It had been a great day in Ontario with my good friend, Mikey. But now Coyotee Boy was on my mind, and I thought about him a lot as we made our way back home to Clinton County.

Ignorance of the law excuses no man; not that all men know the law, but because 'tis an excuse every man will plead, and no man can tell how to confute him.
~John Seldon Table-Talk "Law" Circa 1600

The Silver Fox

MARCH OFTEN FINDS ME CONTENDING with court trials for violations that occurred during the prior hunting season. Most Game Law violations are classed as summary offenses and are heard before local district judges. The game warden is the prosecutor, and must be very familiar with the rules of criminal procedure. The officer also needs to be aware of existing appellate court decisions that may affect how the judge will rule.

In many of these trials, the defendant will be represented by an attorney. A good defense attorney gives the defendant a tremendous edge in the courtroom. The game warden prosecuting a case must be well prepared in order to win a battle of wits with a sharp attorney. Overwhelming evidence of a violation may not be enough to convict if a defense attorney can persuade the judge a procedural error had been made.

At a summary trial, guilt must be proven beyond a reasonable doubt. However, this does not mean that guilt must be established beyond all doubt, or to a mathematical certainty. Many Game Law violations are won in the courtroom by circumstantial evidence alone. I remember one such case where I was able to prove that the defendant had killed three deer during the same hunting license year, even though I could only produce the carcass of one deer as evidence. It was the 1978 antlerless deer season and hunters were only permitted one deer per year, either a buck or doe.

Sylvester Fox didn't really care much about rules, regulations and laws. When it came to hunting, he did whatever it took to be successful, and he did it often. Sylvester's nickname was Sly, aka "The Silver Fox." He had long, silver-gray hair pulled back into a ponytail, and the tip of his "tail" fell halfway down his back. He was a tall, handsome man and very proud of the length of his hair. Sly was single, and I would often see him accompanied by a beautiful woman when he was in town. There's no doubt the ladies were attracted to him, and he believed that was because of his long flowing ponytail and its unusual color. Sly would pull the ponytail over his shoulder and gently stroke it during conversations with people. He certainly did stand out in a crowd, but this tall, dark and handsome man had one major flaw: He was an alcoholic.

I remember walking into the Renovo YMCA restaurant on a beautiful sunny afternoon during the mid-summer of 1977. As I made my way to a table near a window, I noticed Sly out of the corner of my eye. It was his silvery hair that made him stand out, even though he was slumped over on the table. A bowl of stew was tipped over near the top of his head, and a waitress was on her way over to clean it up.

I sat down and soon Isabelle, my favorite waitress, came over to my table. She was a small thin woman in her mid-fifties with black hair beginning to turn gray.

"What are you having today, John?" she asked with her usual bright smile.

"How about a grilled cheese sandwich and a glass of water."

"You betcha," she replied. That's one of the reasons she was my favorite. She always answered with "you betcha." And then she would holler to the cook, "Grilled cheese for John," as though the cook should know to make it special for John, whichever John that may be.

"What's up with Sly?" I asked.

"He fell asleep again."

"Again?"

"You betcha. He falls asleep and we can't wake him," she replied with a tone of despair.

"Is he all right?" I asked.

"You betcha. When he's been drinking, sometimes he'll doze off in the middle of a meal!"

"And you can't wake him?"

"Nope, no matter how hard we try. We just gotta let him sleep it off, and then he gets up, pays his bill and leaves. Funny thing is that when he wakes up, he doesn't seem drunk because his gait is normal and so is his speech."

"That's kind of strange, isn't it?"

"You betcha."

What a shame, I thought. I knew Sly had a reputation as an outlaw hunter, but it was sad to see him like that.

Several months later, I saw Sly again. It was the fall turkey season, and I caught him hunting from a baited blind. Turkey blinds were illegal, and so was the use of bait. We made arrangements to meet a few days later, and Sly paid his fine with a field acknowledgement of guilt. As I was filling out the official receipt, Sly interrupted.

"This won't stop me!" He barked.

"Thanks for the warning."

"I'm serious. You can fine me, you can take my license, but I will always hunt turkeys this way."

"Well that's too bad, because most hunters obey game laws."

"Well I ain't most hunters!"

So it wasn't until the antlerless deer season of 1978 that I would see the Silver Fox again. I was on a remote mountaintop along Pete's Run Road in the heart of the Sproul State Forest District. Sproul is the largest state forest tract in the Commonwealth, containing more than 300,000 acres, or about 475 square miles of woodland. It is mostly made up of steep and rugged sidehills cut by tributaries of the West Branch of the Susquehanna River. The Sproul is one of several adjoining state forest districts in northcentral Pennsylvania that make up more than 1.5 million acres of public land.

The antlerless deer season was about to end; it was almost sunset, the second and final day of "doe" season, and only minutes remained for a licensed hunter to take their season limit of one deer.

Sylvester Fox was having a great day, a great season for that matter. However, all great things must come to an end, as Sly was about to discover. When I came upon The Silver Fox, he was on his way home from hunting. We were approaching each other on a very narrow portion of a dirt road, and Sly pulled over and stopped in order to let me get by. However, instead of driving around him, I stopped beside his truck, rolled down my window, and looked directly at Sly. He looked straight ahead as though he didn't notice me, so I waited. In a moment, he rolled down his window and turned his head toward me.

"Any luck?" I asked.

"Yep," was all he said. I glanced over toward the bed of his truck and could see a deer.

"I think I'll have a look at it."

"It's a doe!" he snapped at me. "You can see it just fine from where you are!"

"Shut your engine off," I said, as I exited my patrol vehicle and walked over to the back of his truck. The deer was "tagged" with the required portion of his hunting license detached and affixed to its ear. However, I noticed a lot of blood on the tag, and when I see a blood-soaked deer tag, I immediately take a closer look. Sometimes, when an unscrupulous hunter uses his tag more than one time, he will smear it with blood to obscure the original information written on it. As I removed the tag to examine it more closely, Sly got out of his truck and walked over with a concerned look on his face.

During the 1970s, hunting licenses and the attached deer tags were nothing more than a heavy gauge of paper, and tags could easily be altered. The tag was designed so that it could be used on either an antlerless or antlered deer. On the lower right portion of the detachable deer tag was a section for the successful hunter to fill in the number of points for an antlered deer. The hunter was to include the number of points for each antler, and the total points. Just beside that section, there was a block marked "male" and a block marked "female," and the successful hunter was to check off the appropriate block.

Date Killed	Time Killed	**DEER TAG**	
		ANTLERLESS PERMIT #	
County in which killed		# _____	
		ACTUAL NUMBER OF POINTS EACH ANTLER	SEX
Hunter's Name		RIGHT ANTLER _____	
		LEFT ANTLER _____	☐ MALE
ADDRESS		TOTAL _____	☐ FEMALE

When filling out the tag for an antlerless deer, a hunter would leave the right antler and left antler portion blank or write a zero for each. However, in this instance a number "1" appeared to have been filled in for both the right and the left antler, and I could see a number "2" filled in for the total points. The block marked "male" had been faintly filled in with a check mark, while the block marked "female" was empty.

I told Sly that I was certain he had used the tag previously on a spike buck. I explained his right to a hearing, and gave him an opportunity to confess and pay the penalty by way of a field acknowledgment of guilt. Sly claimed that he was innocent, and that I didn't know what I was talking about. All the while, he had his ponytail pulled over his right shoulder, gently stroking it with his left hand.

"I have a friend who practices law in Philadelphia," he said. "He will make a fool out of you in front of any judge."

"Okay, guess I'll see you in court."

"Suits me just fine," Sly said with a broad grin.

"Just be aware it may take some time before I file charges," I told him.

"Why's that…I got you worried?"

"Not at all. You will be hearing from me as soon as the Pennsylvania State Police Crime Lab finishes analyzing your deer tag." My mention of the Crime Lab caused Sly's confident expression to disappear as fast as turning off a light switch. I removed the doe from his pickup truck for evidence, gave him a receipt, and told him he could leave.

"How about my deer!" he demanded.

"It's evidence, so it stays with me."

About five weeks later, I received the report from the Crime Lab. Trooper Lawrence Herb, a documents examiner for the Pennsylvania State Police, had done an excellent job of deciphering the bloodstained deer tag. He used microscopic examinations and infrared photography to detect what had been written on the tag. Trooper Herb was able to determine that the "right antler" section actually had had two entries filled in: a number three with a number one written over it. The "left antler" section also had two entries: a number two with a number one written over it. The block marked "total" for total points had two entries: a number five, with a number two written over it. The tag clearly had been used for two antlered deer, a five-point buck and a spike buck before being placed on the doe.

The following day, I filed citations against Sly for killing two deer over the limit and for transporting a doe improperly tagged. Sly pleaded not guilty and a summary trial was scheduled for mid-March before a district judge in Renovo. Sly was accompanied by an attorney when his day in court finally arrived, and he seemed confident of being found not guilty. However, they didn't know I would have a State Police Crime Lab scientist at the trial from the Bureau of Forensic Services. They make their facilities available to the Game Commission, and with their assistance, we have been able to solve many complex cases over the years.

When Trooper Herb began to testify for the Commonwealth, I could see that Sly was starting to worry. When an infrared photograph of his deer tag (enlarged to eight times its original size) was introduced as evidence, Sly began checking to see if his shoes were tied. He was found guilty of all the charges I filed against him, fined several hundred dollars, and had his hunting and trapping privileges revoked for three years. The Philadelphia defense attorney was very impressed with our evidence. I'm sure Sly felt foolish when his attorney asked for a copy of one of the infrared photographs to show to his attorney friends as a conversation piece. The attorney had traveled to the big woods of Clinton County thinking he would easily prevail. He traveled back to the city with a newfound respect for game wardens and state troopers.

It would be almost three years until our paths crossed once again. There was an illegal turkey blind in the vicinity of where I had caught him with the doe. The blind was on a ridge top between Barney Run and the West Branch of the Susquehanna River. It had been built with tree limbs and logs in an open area of large timber. I first came upon it while on foot patrol shortly after the close of the 1978 turkey season. During the 1979 turkey season, I made several trips to the blind, but it always seemed that I was a day late. Fresh candy wrappers and cigarette butts in the blind were all I would find for my trouble. The ground surrounding the blind was heavily baited with wheat and cracked corn. A flock of turkeys was habituated to working the bait, and I can remember scattering the birds on numerous occasions while walking in on the blind. The 1980 turkey season came and went with the same results, and I wondered if I was ever going to catch the guilty party. The 1981 turkey season ended with no results after several hikes to the blind, and it had become a real thorn in my side.

It was the Friday before buck season, six days after the turkey season closed, when I decided to check the blind one last time. I never walked in on it during the closed season, and I thought it was worth a try. It was early in the afternoon when I entered the woods near the blind. I noticed a car about a quarter mile up the road, but dismissed it as probably belonging to a squirrel hunter. As I approached the blind, I could sense that something was different. At first, I wasn't sure what it was, but something looked out of place. When I got closer, it appeared that a stick was poking out of the blind. That was it! That's what was different! As I continued toward the blind at a faster pace the "stick" transformed into a shotgun barrel.

When I reached the blind, my heart was racing. I didn't know what to expect from the person I was about to confront while alone in a remote section of forest. I cautiously peered inside the blind and saw the Silver Fox. He was sound asleep!

At first, I was going to wake him, but then I remembered what Isabelle told me a few years ago: *He falls asleep and we can't wake him no matter how hard we try. We just gotta let him sleep it off.* And I recalled Sly telling me he would never quit hunting turkeys from a baited blind. So now what? Would anything be accomplished with another fine and license revocation? Sly was still on revocation from the deer case! I thought about it for a while and came up with a plan of action. But first, I unloaded Sly's ten-gauge double barrel shotgun, put both rounds in my pocket, and laid the shotgun on the ground outside of the blind. Then I began the hike back to my patrol vehicle for a tool that would be helpful.

As I jogged through the woods, my mind went back to the night I first met the Silver Fox. It was March 1976, a time when the forest begins to thaw after a long cold winter. The weather can vary from extreme cold one day to balmy warmth the next. As the frost line begins to dissipate, falling rocks become a common occurrence along roadways here, and I would stop and remove them whenever possible.

Route 120 begins near Lock Haven and runs through Clinton, Cameron and Elk County ending at Ridgway. This two-lane highway is the most heavily traveled road in my patrol district. It winds through steep, narrow valleys paralleling the West Branch of the Susquehanna River and the Sinnemahoning Creek. It was known as the Bucktail Trail in the 1860s, named after a famous Civil War regiment called the Bucktail Rangers. Prior to that, it was called the Sinnema-honing Trail, and was used by Indians traveling between the Susquehanna and Allegheny Rivers. This 75-mile length of highway and the adjacent land from mountain rim to mountain rim is now known as Bucktail State Park. It is mostly forested, with Renovo (population 1,100) being the largest town between Lock Haven and Emporium. When the road was built here some 100 years ago, mountain walls in the narrower passages of the river valley had to be blasted away to clear a right-of-way. As a result, sheer rock walls meet the very edge of the highway. Locally they are referred to as "cuts." Many of them have been named, such as the Ritchie Cut and the Ice Mine Cut. It is these cuts that give Route 120 its reputation as a potentially dangerous highway. The Ice Mine Cut is located about five miles above Lock Haven, and it was long known for rock landslides until a mitigation project cut the hillside back from the roadway in 1997.

Late one night in March 1976, I came upon a rockslide at the Ice Mine Cut that completely blocked Route 120. I was off duty and traveling from Lock Haven to Renovo in my personal vehicle. The boulders were piled six feet high in the center of the highway. There were rocks from the mountain wall all the way across both lanes to the opposite shoulder. It was very late at night, so it would be quite a while before the highway department could get any heavy equipment to the area. Fortunately, the rocks were not piled up as high on the shoulder. A detour would have meant traveling 25 extra miles on dirt roads, so I decided to try clearing off an area wide enough to get my vehicle around the slide. The arduous task of lifting the rocks and dropping them over the guide rail soon had me wishing someone else would happen upon the scene.

It wasn't long before I heard a vehicle approaching from the opposite side of the slide, and it sounded like it was traveling at a high rate of speed. I dropped the rock I was holding and picked up my flashlight. Suddenly I could see the vehicle's headlights as it broke over a rise in the roadway about two hundred yards away. The driver didn't see the rockslide! It was right there in front of him, a huge rock wall, and he didn't see it! I frantically waved my flashlight in a futile attempt to warn him, but the vehicle continued to race toward the massive stone wall. At the last moment, I ran for cover and ducked behind my vehicle.

The driver never had a chance to use his brakes and struck the stone barrier at 60 miles per hour! I ran up to the rockslide, fully expecting the worst. I couldn't believe it; the car was resting on top of the rock pile with its wheels at eye level! I hollered up to the occupants and prayed for a response that they were okay. The driver's door slowly opened and the bewildered occupant looked down at me with an expression of shock. It was the Silver Fox.

"What did I hit?" he groaned. Miraculously, Sly and the three ladies with him were not injured. I helped them get out of the car and down the rockslide to the roadway. Soon more vehicles arrived, and I had plenty of help removing rocks from the road. The driver of the first vehicle heading toward Lock Haven offered to contact the highway department and State Police.

With the aid of two men from approaching vehicles, I was able to clear the shoulder of rocks and make a passageway for vehicles to get by the slide. The bright headlights and taillights from Sly's car perched on top of the rock pile was a clear warning for approaching vehicles. It took the better part of the following day for the highway department to remove the rockslide and get the highway completely safe for motorists.

I could see the outline of my patrol vehicle just ahead, so I slowed down from a jog to a brisk walk. When I arrived at the Ford Bronco, the first thing I did was reach for my thermos for a refreshing drink of water. Next, I grabbed my heavy-duty Cutco shears and about twelve inches of bailing twine. Then I made an about-face and jogged back toward the baited blind.

Within 200 yards of the blind, I slowed to a quiet walk, and soon I could see that the shotgun was still lying outside of the blind. Then I could hear Sly snoring. He was still out like a light. When I reached the blind and looked inside, I could see that he hadn't moved a muscle. Sly was slumped over and lying with his face pointed away from me. His long ponytail was stretched out on the ground and flowing in my direction, so I grabbed the shears tucked inside my belt.

No, I can't do it, I thought…At least not all of it. I stepped inside the blind and grabbed the bottom of his ponytail in my fist. The silver-gray ponytail had some white hair running through it; quite unusual I said to myself. Then, just above my fist, I cut off the last four inches of his tail.

I snapped a small branch off a nearby tree and tied Sly's lock of hair to it with a nice, neat bowtie. Then I pushed the branch into the ground between the blind and the bait. It would be the first thing Sly saw when he woke up.

As I jogged back to my patrol vehicle, I suddenly remembered who owned the car that was parked up the road. It belonged to Sly's girlfriend! He must have used her car thinking I wouldn't recognize it, and I didn't until that moment. I went directly to it on my way back and placed both of his shotgun shells on the hood of her car. Then I hiked the short distance to my Bronco and headed out of the area to continue my patrol. I returned the next day and tore the blind apart, scattering it across the forest floor.

Sly quit drinking alcohol and started attending Alcoholics Anonymous meetings in Lock Haven. He quit hunting turkeys from baited blinds too. Losing part of his ponytail was like losing his brand, his identification. He also realized how vulnerable his alcoholism made him. I think he knew that I was the person who cut off part of his ponytail, but he never confronted me about it. Perhaps he was just so embarrassed about his drunken stupor that he wanted to pretend it didn't happen. His ponytail grew back and reached its full length in a little over one year. The Silver Fox was reborn a better man!

I never found the companion that was so companionable as solitude.
~Henry David Thoreau

The Blade

As THE MONTH OF MARCH FADES AWAY, the warm April sun breathes new life into my rugged and remote patrol district. I begin thinking about the upcoming trout season and the spring gobbler season that will soon follow. It is the trout season that I most anxiously await, as the pristine beauty of my favorite trout stream beckons my return. Each spring, my son John Jr. and I reacquaint ourselves with a beautiful, isolated mountain stream not far from my home. The water is pure, cold and crystal clear, often belying its true depth. Some of the deeper pools exceed five feet, yet every pebble and piece of forest debris that make up the streambed can be distinctly seen. We never bother to pack anything to drink, only food, as there is nothing sweeter than the water from this secluded wilderness trout stream.

The native brook trout we catch here are the most brightly colored I have ever seen, and a limit of these delectable beauties is not difficult to come by for the experienced angler. My son and I have never met another person while fishing this stream, and we normally cover a distance of several miles. The inaccessibility of this waterway preserves its primitive beauty and abundance of native brook trout.

Aldo Leopold declared in his masterwork *A Sand County Almanac,* that waters play their own song on rock, root, and rapids. He went on to write, "It is a pleasant music, bespeaking dancing riffles." Then he warned that the song of a pristine stream may cause a natural park to be designated, "to bring the music to the many, but by the time the many are attuned to hear it, there is little left but noise." So I will keep the location of this pristine mountain stream a secret, known only to my son and me.

The author (right) and his son along their secret mountain stream.

The opening day of spring gobbler season follows closely on the heels of the beginning of trout season. Few experiences can match the thrill of calling in a handsome, robust gobbler as it struts majestically on the forest floor, ever ready to escape at the slightest sign of danger.

Spring hunting for these elusive birds is restricted to calling only, and only birds with a visible beard may be taken. However, even with these restrictions, a hunter will sometimes be shot in mistake for a wild turkey.

Many times the offending hunter is stalking what he thinks is a bird, even though regulations prohibit stalking and require calling the gobbler in to the hunter's location. A hunter dressed in camouflage in order to blend in with his surroundings, while imitating the sound of a turkey, puts himself in a vulnerable position.

While it is recommended that some fluorescent orange material be displayed while calling, many hunters fail to do this. Wrapping a fluorescent orange band around a tree or hanging a blaze orange cap or vest from an overhead branch could prevent an accident. It is movement, not color, that will spook a wild turkey. A safety measure such as this certainly would have prevented the following accident that I investigated many years ago.

Harry was sitting under a large hemlock tree dressed in full camouflage. He thought he was well concealed under the shadow of the tree. However, the back side of his hunting license holder was bright red, similar to a spring gobbler's head and neck. And unbeknownst to him, the license holder had flipped up displaying the red color.

Bob and Pete were walking single-file down a trail behind Harry just as he let out a few yelps from his turkey call. Bob was in the lead, acting as a guide for Pete. Both of them heard the yelps and immediately froze in their tracks, as they believed the sound came from a hen turkey just ahead. Suddenly, Bob spotted the red license holder on Harry's back.

"There's a gobbler in full strut under that hemlock just ahead!" he whispered. Bob saw what he wanted to see, even though Harry didn't look anything like a wild turkey. Bob quickly stepped to his left and dropped to his knees while pointing toward the hemlock tree. Pete cautiously walked toward the tree while raising his 12 gauge shotgun.

Harry heard something behind him, and slowly began to turn around. His heart stopped when he saw the shotgun pointed directly at him, but before he could utter a sound, three blasts from the gun ripped into his body. He was hit in the face, chest, both arms, and his left leg with number six birdshot pellets. The force of the impact sent him backwards and down on the ground hard. He lost consciousness for a moment. Bob and Pete were shocked, as both of them thought Harry was a gobbler "in full strut." They were experienced hunters and couldn't believe what happened. Pete's knees weakened and he felt like he was about to vomit. Seeing Harry lying on the ground instead of a turkey seemed impossible. Then reality set in. They had to get Harry to the hospital, if he was still alive. When Harry groaned, Pete and Bob bolted to his side. They managed to get him out of the woods and transported to the Bucktail Medical Center in Renovo. Harry was seriously wounded but survived thanks to the heavy coat he was wearing.

I interviewed everyone, and Pete admitted he mistook the red license holder for the head and neck of a gobbler. I filed charges of shooting and wounding a human in mistake for a wild turkey and he pleaded guilty. He was fined several hundred dollars and had his hunting privileges revoked for a period of five years by the Clinton County Court of Common Pleas. The fact that both hunters mistook the victim for a turkey "in full strut" sets this hunting accident apart from the many I have investigated.

Hunting accident investigations are one of the most unpleasant duties game wardens must perform. Our job involves a lot more than sleeping under a star-lit sky and catching our breakfast from an icy stream, as some magazine advertisements would like their readers to believe. Sometimes we must deal with individuals that are worse than picking up a dozen dripping, maggot-infested roadkilled deer during a heat wave in July. In my 34 years with the Game Commission, there is one person who surpassed all others in such a comparison.

Vito "The Blade" was a dangerous man. He had a record of 35 adult criminal arrests with 23 convictions when I had my first confrontation with him many years ago. I was a prosecution witness in an upcoming trial where serious criminal charges had been filed against him for threatening a county district judge. The judge was accosted in front of his home while Vito was holding a box containing a handgun. A fistful of bullets was shoved in the judge's face while intimidating threats were delivered in a burst of abusive profanity. The charges of terroristic threats, harassment, conspiracy, and driving while license suspended were subsequently filed against Vito. And Vito, true to form, counter-filed charges against the judge. He met with the County District Attorney and claimed the judge grabbed him around the throat and tried to choke him. And this occurred, according to Vito, during an argument about Vito's girlfriend.

I was asked to be a character witness for the judge and readily consented. I knew the judge, and like most people, he wasn't going to start a fight with "The Blade." Vito's story about an argument over his girlfriend was ridiculous. Because of typical small town gossip, Vito soon learned that I was going to be a witness in court, so he waited for an opportunity to persuade me to have a change of heart.

On February 12, 1981 while I was off duty and unarmed, Vito confronted me in the lobby of the YMCA in Renovo. I was there for a workout and about to go downstairs to a weight room in the basement. There were no other people in the lobby when Vito and I came face to face. Although Vito was not large in stature, what he lacked in size he made up for in reckless audacity. He blocked my path and made a veiled threat concerning my health. Then he told me that I should stay out of his business concerning the judge, and that was immediately followed by a tirade of vulgarities.

"Move out of my way!" I warned him. "You're blocking my path."

"You don't scare me," he said.

"If I was trying to scare you, you'd be lying on the floor," I said."

"Yeah right. Better watch your back," he huffed while turning away to walk into the dining room.

I went downstairs and walked by the bowling lanes. There were a dozen bowlers there and many of them were smoking, so I held my breath and quickly turned into the weight room. I changed clothes in the locker room and started warming up on the bench press with a light barbell. Mikey was there, but I didn't say anything to him about Vito. I finished my first warmup set and sat upright on the bench. That's when I noticed Mikey staring toward the doorway. I turned and saw Vito standing there. He didn't say anything. He just stared at me with his right arm stuffed in his coat pocket.

"Hey Vito, long time no see," I said sarcastically.

"The next time you see me could be your last," he whispered just loud enough that Mikey couldn't hear him.

"John, is everything okay?" Mikey asked. I turned toward Mikey and told him everything was just fine. Then I looked back at Vito.

"Vito, how much do you weigh?" Vito didn't say anything, he just stared, and I could sense that Mikey was getting nervous. And so was I. Guys like Vito only understood the law of the jungle, eat or be eaten, the superiority of brute force.

"Well let me guess," I said. "Maybe 180 pounds or so." Still no reply from Vito. Meanwhile Mikey made his way over by my side. I had 135 pounds loaded on the barbell, so I put another 25 pounds on each end.

"Vito, this barbell is loaded with 185 pounds, why don't you step in and workout with us." Mikey was watching Vito guardedly as I got into position by lying back on the bench. Then I started banging out repetitions with the barbell. I brought it down to my chest and straight up, briefly locking my elbows before the next repetition. When I got to 25 reps, Vito turned and walked away. I racked the barbell, stood up and looked at Mikey. Both of us were smiling ear to ear. We raised arms and smacked palms for a high five. Then we started laughing, and any stress either of us had was gone at that moment.

The following morning Trooper Steve Toboz, a criminal investigator from the Lamar barracks, met me in Renovo. We agreed that charges of attempting to intimidate a witness and harassment should be filed against Vito. Vito happened to see me talking to the trooper, and correctly assumed that he was the subject of our conversation. He then went to the same district judge he had threatened, and demanded that charges be filed against me, claiming I had pointed a gun at him in the lobby of the YMCA. The judge handed him a private complaint form and told him to fill it out himself. Vito shook his head and stormed out of the building, mumbling something about not knowing how to write.

About one month later, it was Vito's day in court concerning the district judge he threatened. The night before the trial, the prosecuting district attorney received an anonymous phone call from someone who threatened to kill him if he continued with the case.

When Vito walked into the courtroom, everyone noticed the expensive suit and flashy gold jewelry he wore. He stood beside his attorney and stared at each member of the jury in a contemptuous bid of defiance. He then looked at his victim, the district judge, and shook his head in disgust. If he were to be tried on appearances alone, there would have been no need for the Commonwealth to present its case. In just a few brief moments Vito managed to alienate those very people who were about to decide his fate.

As it turned out, I was never called to the witness stand. When Vito testified, he tarnished his image and impeached his credibility to such an extent that it wasn't necessary. He testified that the district judge, in previous encounters, asked him to throw paint on a car owned by a tenant he wasn't able to evict. Then he testified the judge wanted him to burn down a camp belonging to a contractor who messed up a job for his father. Vito stated the judge asked him to beat up a man who was harassing his family. He swore the judge asked him to burn down a home because the occupant threw acid on his house. Vito said the judge asked him to beat up two men because they were calling him at all hours of the night. He testified the judge asked him to get another man "out of the way" whom he'd put in jail a few times. Vito said he was asked to beat up another man because he burned a paper bag and set off M-80 explosives on the judge's porch. He also testified the judge asked him to burn down his own cabin so he could collect the insurance. And to top it all off, Vito testified that the judge asked his girlfriend out on a date. I sat there in utter amazement as I listened to his lies. Who would be crazy enough to ask this guy's girlfriend out on a date!

All of these requests had allegedly been made over a period of two or three years, but Vito claimed he didn't commit any of those crimes. The district attorney asked him why the judge would continue to ask for favors when Vito kept refusing. Vito said he didn't know.

The jury deliberated for several hours and found Vito guilty of terroristic threats and criminal conspiracy. He was subsequently released on bail pending his sentencing, and it was during that time that the incident between us at the YMCA went before the court. I was called to the witness stand first, and testified about what had taken place that night in the lobby.

When Vito took the stand. He declared that it was I who confronted him. He testified that I accused him of poaching deer, and tried to start a fight because I wasn't smart enough to catch him. Vito even arranged for reporters to be present from both county newspapers.

"Even if I was poaching deer, there's not a man among you wardens good enough to catch me," he scoffed. When he was finished testifying, a friend of his, Rocco "The Mule" corroborated the entire tale. Rocco testified that he witnessed the event, and agreed with Vito's version. This was completely unexpected. There was no way I could prove that Rocco was lying. It was two against one, and I was concerned that the judge might believe their story.

After postponing his decision for several tense days, the district judge found Vito guilty of harassing me and set a stiff fine. Several weeks later, Vito was summoned to court for sentencing on the terroristic threats and conspiracy convictions concerning the judge. While sentencing Vito, Judge Fink noted his criminal record.

"The common golden thread that is evident is a disregard of law and order," the judge stated. Judge Fink then read out loud a long list of prior convictions.

"Young man, you've been speeding all your life, in and out of a motor vehicle," he declared. "I get the idea you live within a law unto yourself...and this is judgment day!"

Vito was sentenced to one to three years in prison. He spent about six months behind bars before his attorney managed to have him released on bail pending an appeal of his sentence. While he was out on bail, Vito was required to maintain his former out-of-state residence in Connecticut. He was also instructed, as a condition of his bail, that a violation of any state law would not be tolerated by the court.

Several months later, while Vito was still out on bail, I received unconfirmed information that he moved back to Pennsylvania and was staying with Rocco in Bucks County. My brother, Bill was serving as the state game warden in neighboring Montgomery County at the time (he eventually transferred to Wyoming County). I called Bill and filled him in with the information I had. Vito liked venison, and poaching a deer at night with a spotlight was his modus operandi. Bill said he would be on the lookout, and he put the word out to the game wardens stationed in neighboring districts.

I'll never forget the telephone call I got from my brother a few weeks later. When I answered the phone he said, "John, we got him!" He didn't have to say who.

On November 17 1982, State Game Warden Cheryl Trewella apprehended Vito and Rocco jacklighting a deer in her Bucks County district. Cheryl was the first female to become a Pennsylvania state game warden, and she had graduated from our training school only five months earlier. I remembered what Vito said in the courtroom and chuckled. *There's not a man among you wardens good enough to catch me!* Well, he called that one right, I thought. Both men pleaded guilty, never realizing that Cheryl knew Vito was out on bail, and that she intended to contact me.

As soon as I was given all the details, I contacted the county district attorney's office. Vito was subsequently ordered back to the county court house for a hearing concerning his two bail-condition violations. State Game Warden Trewella and I appeared at the courthouse for the hearing, and it was obvious that Vito was unnerved. However, he still managed to give us a menacing glare as we entered the courtroom. After all the evidence was presented to the judge, Vito's bail was immediately revoked, and he was sent back to jail that same afternoon.

Six years later, Vito and I came face to face again. I was driving my patrol vehicle on Young Woman's Creek Road during the opening day of doe season. The road was a solid sheet of ice, and I was running a bit late to meet up with Ranger. I rounded a curve and saw a man of hulking, well-fed girth standing on the edge of the road ahead of me. It was Rocco. He bent over, grabbed a small deer by the hind leg, and began to drag it across the road. When he saw my vehicle, he hastily tried to cross the roadway, but began slipping on the ice. I applied my brakes, but to no avail, as my vehicle began sliding and fishtailing. I countersteered and regained partial control but was still sliding as I slammed my palm to the horn in a frantic attempt to alert Rocco of his impending doom. At the last instant, he dropped the deer in the middle of the road, and it seemed as though he was running on a treadmill as his legs kept moving while he remained in place. Curly, of the *Three Stooges*, couldn't have done it better.

There was nothing I could do to prevent running over the deer and crushing its hindquarters. *I can't be this unlucky*, I muttered to myself. The thought of having to deal with Rocco after squashing his deer made me cringe. Only Vito would have been worse to deal with when humble pie was on the menu. I finally got my Chevy Blazer stopped and then backed up to the mangled deer. When I walked around to the back of the vehicle, I was shocked to see that my luck had indeed hit bottom. There was Vito, dressed in fluorescent orange and leaning against a tree on the opposite side of the narrow road. He was wearing a gold necklace with a large gold pendant, a thick gold bracelet, and three gold rings studded with diamonds.

"Why the heck did you run over my deer!" he shouted angrily.

"It was either Rocco or the deer," I said, "so I thought about it and chose the deer." I knew that answer wasn't going to satisfy Vito. I glanced down to the deer's head and saw that it hadn't been tagged, and breathed a sigh of relief. I was never very good at being humble.

"The deer belongs to the Commonwealth now," I informed him. "You didn't tag it."

"So what! It's no good anyhow, you ran over it!" he boomed.

Then I told Vito that I was also going to cite him, and the fine amounted to $100. With that he came apart at the seams and went into a frenzied, ranting discourse of profanities.

Like a man possessed, he rambled on and on, screaming and shouting at the top of his lungs. Rocco was doing his best to calm him down, but it was useless. Vito's voice rolled off the steep mountain walls surrounding us. He brought up the past and claimed that was why I was arresting him.

I did my best to ignore him while I loaded the deer onto my vehicle, and then began filling out a citation. After a while, Vito finally calmed down and started pacing back and forth as he waited for me to finish writing. I also wrote two warnings: one for failure to display his doe license as required, and another for failure to sign it. I handed him the warnings first, and told him that he was being treated the same as anyone else. I explained that I was not going to allow our troubled past to influence how I would treat him, and reminded him that the warnings could just as easily have been citations.

Vito's entire demeanor changed. I think it was the written warnings that did it. He pulled a large roll of money out of his pocket and peeled off five $20 bills. After I gave him a field receipt for the cash, he started to grin.

"You know," he said, "it's really kind of funny when you think about it. First you run over my deer, then you make me pay a hundred bucks for it... and I don't even get to keep it." With that he began to laugh. It was sort of a wild, hysterical laugh. Rocco looked confused at first, but he knew if Vito laughed, he'd better be laughing along with him as a sign of respect—or maybe it was fear. They were still laughing as I got into my vehicle and pulled away.

As I drove down the icy mountain road with Vito's squashed deer dangling from my deer rack, I realized that he taught me something valuable that day: gold clashes terribly with fluorescent orange.

> *Note: I never saw Vito again. However, three years later he was apprehended in Hyner (Clinton County) after a high-speed chase that involved several law enforcement agencies. On April 16, 1991, Vito fired two shots from a rifle, breaking the front and rear windows of a van owned by a man and woman he was threatening. A PA State Trooper arrived on the scene located at a bar near Lock Haven, prompting Vito to jump in his car and speed away. While the trooper was in pursuit, he radioed ahead for a roadblock to be set up. Vito drove through the roadblock, and then other officers joined in the chase. The 20-mile pursuit ended when he was finally stopped a considerable distance from the roadblock. Vito was charged with driving while intoxicated, terroristic threats, recklessly endangering others, criminal mischief and several other complaints. He was placed in Clinton County Prison after his arraignment.*

Later that day, Ranger contacted me by two-way radio about an investigation we needed to do, and was waiting on the porch when I pulled into the driveway. He stepped off the porch, sprinted to my patrol vehicle, and hopped inside.

"What's going on?" I asked.

"I was gonna ask the same question, what the heck happened to that deer?"

"I'll tell you on the way, you won't believe it. Now where are we going and why?" Ranger told me he received a phone call from a bartender in Renovo. The bartender found three dead deer in the back yard of the bar when he took the trash out that morning. When we arrived, the bar had just opened for business. It was early, so the place was empty. The bartender, Joey, was visibly shaken when we walked inside.

"Look, I don't want any trouble," he said, "but this is crazy. They had to have been killed last night." Joey asked us to follow him out back, where three doe were lying on the ground, all of them shot in the head with a small caliber bullet.

"Do you have any idea who could have done this?" I asked while staring straight into his eyes. Joey hesitated for a moment, and then he looked down at the ground. "Nope!" he answered.

"Come on Joey, I think you have an idea who did this. You have my word; anything you say will be confidential."

"Promise?" he asked, his voice trembling. Ranger and I both nodded affirmatively.

"Coyotee Boy…I think it was Coyotee Boy. Look, if he thinks I ratted on him my bar will burn to the ground!"

"He won't suspect you; I'll make sure of it."

Joey said that Coyotee Boy was at the bar that night, drinking heavily, and when Joey finally cut him off, he became enraged. "He stormed out of my bar, but not before tearing up the petition and scattering it on the floor."

"What petition?" I asked.

"I had a petition to abolish doe season. It had a bunch of signatures and I was gonna send it to the Game Commission."

"So you think he was sending you a message; is that it?"

"Yep, he wouldn't sign it. He said he kills whatever he wants." According to Joey, there were no other customers when Coyotee Boy had his temper tantrum and stormed out of the bar. I thanked Joey for the information, and then we loaded the carcasses on the deer rack attached to the back of my truck.

Later that day, we were able to recover a .22 caliber bullet from each of two deer. The third doe had been shot from the side, with the bullet passing through each eye. That was a Coyotee Boy trademark. He often bragged about the skill it took for that kind of shot, and how it removed any opportunity for a ballistics examination. However, one of the bullets was in great condition for ballistics, and I was certain Coyotee Boy possessed the matching rifle. Unfortunately, I didn't have enough evidence to get a search warrant for his gun.

I remembered what Mikey told me at the Police Olympics in Ottawa. Maybe Coyotee Boy was right, I thought. Maybe I'll never catch him. I quickly dismissed that thought and put the badly damaged bullet in the ashtray of my patrol vehicle. The other one went to the evidence locker. The bullet inside the ashtray would bounce and rattle around while driving on most of the roads in my district, and after a while it would get a little annoying. However, I decided it would stay there as a constant reminder to catch Coyotee Boy, no matter how long it took.

The woods are lovely, dark and deep
But I have promises to keep,
And miles to go before I sleep,
    ~ Robert Frost

And Miles to Go Before I Sleep

IT WAS AN EXCEPTIONALLY MILD NIGHT in May 1989 as I slowly raised the cup to my mouth and took a sip of hot black coffee. I set the cup down on a small shallow saucer and listened to it vibrate as a massive 200 ton locomotive groaned to a stop just outside the door of Socky's Restaurant. Renovo is an old railroad town, so most of the businesses, including Socky's, are located on a one way street that parallels the tracks. The reverberating idle of the immense engine rattled every window in the building, and the stool I was seated on began to shimmy. An old lanky railroader climbed down out of the locomotive and walked across the street, brushing off his trousers with his hat as he entered the eatery.

"Three coffees to go," he said as he glanced at me seated at the end of the counter. His eyes were still squinting from the bright lights inside as he nodded a hello. After being served and paying for the coffee, he walked back out into the warm night air. Moments later, the huge Conrail engine began to move, straining at first due to its enormous weight, and then gradually increasing speed as it departed. I sat there deep in thought as the locomotive's thunderous rolling cadence soon became a distant drumming in the still night air. Perhaps it was this sound that made me think back to an incident that occurred on November 14, 1977 along a different portion of the railroad.

I was having lunch at the YMCA restaurant in Renovo when the cashier, who was also the police dispatcher, called me over to the telephone. The person on the phone, Jake, asked me to come to the remote village of Keating right away. Someone had just killed a deer. The big game hunting season hadn't started yet, so I jumped into my patrol car and sped off to the scene, not knowing what to expect when I got there. Within fifteen minutes, I was at the location described over the phone, and introduced myself to Jake. Jake had just retired from the Navy, where he made a career out of training recruits. He was standing next to a 1968 Ford pickup truck that had been abandoned by a young man he encountered earlier. He told me that he watched the man park the truck and enter the woods with a bulging sack in one hand, and a shotgun in the other. Since the man was on Jake's property, he decided to investigate. He soon discovered that the trespasser had deposited the boned out remains of a freshly killed deer under a hemlock tree before continuing on to hunt for grouse.

Jake waited, eventually confronting the culprit as he returned to his pickup truck and demanded to see some identification. The man refused to comply, and tried to step around him. Jake told him that he wasn't going anywhere until the game warden arrived, and insisted that he put his shotgun on the ground. When the man refused, Jake executed a combat disarming technique on the unsuspecting hunter in expert fashion. Like a bolt from the blue, he slammed his rifle into the man's shotgun and knocked it to the ground. The astonished hunter ran over to his pickup truck and jumped inside. But before he could get it started, Jake shouted an ultimatum: If the truck moved, he intended to shoot the tires out. That was when the man bolted from his truck and ran off on foot. He was last seen crossing a nearby bridge that spanned the Sinnemahoning Creek.

Now he was in a virtual no man's land. It is at this location that the Sinnemahoning Creek flows into the west branch of the Susquehanna River. If the man chose to, he could follow the river upstream, walking the railroad for over 20 miles without encountering a single home. And he could do all of this without meeting any roadways, as there are none on either side of the river between Keating, in Clinton County and Karthaus, in Clearfield County. This is a wilderness stretch of river in the truest sense, with only the railroad tracks to assure anyone that civilization does indeed lie somewhere back of beyond. His other choice, and the most logical one, was to take the Sinnemahoning Creek upstream for some 12 miles to the village of Sinnemahoning, in Cameron County. Again he would have to walk the railroad, but the distance to civilization was not nearly so great. His third option was to hide until darkness fell, and then try to sneak back to his truck. So I opened the hood and pulled the distributor cap wire, which would prevent the engine from starting. I decided to hide my vehicle nearby and keep an eye on the truck. I had contacted Ranger earlier, and it wouldn't be long before he came by to assist.

When Ranger arrived, I told him to patrol along the road that parallels the Sinnemahoning Creek, and to watch across the stream for the suspect. I ran a check on the suspect's license plate earlier, and the truck was registered to someone from Weedville. That made the sleepy village of Sinnemahoning a safe bet for the suspect's destination since both villages were in Cameron County.

Ranger was only gone a short period of time when my two-way radio suddenly came to life. His voice cracked through the speaker as he revealed what had just happened. He had spotted the suspect walking along the railroad tracks on the other side of the creek moments earlier. Ranger exited his vehicle and identified himself, shouting for the suspect to stop. But the fugitive just waved a goodbye gesture, and quickly faded into the woods adjacent to the railroad tracks. Now I was confident that the man was headed for Sinnemahoning.

I contacted my neighboring officer, Cameron County Game Warden Norm Erickson, and filled him in on what was going on. I also contacted the Conrail train dispatcher in Renovo and asked him to have trains in the area report any sightings of the suspect. Norm was tied up on an investigation, but he did arrange for a couple of state troopers to watch the railroad tracks near Sinnemahoning.

It was just after sunset when the Conrail dispatcher contacted me. He told me that a locomotive engineer had spotted a person walking along the railroad tracks near Sinnemahoning that fit the suspect's description. I contacted the Pennsylvania State Police substation in Emporium and asked their dispatcher to relay the information to the assisting state troopers. Ranger and I then headed to Sinnemahoning for a rendezvous with the two troopers.

By the time we arrived, it was well past sunset. Deputy Game Warden John Dzemyan (now a retired state game warden), lived in Sinnemahoning and was assisting the state troopers. We were told that the suspect had been spotted just moments earlier, but he disappeared into the darkness when given the command to halt. The five of us searched the densely wooded area by foot, but there was no sign of the suspect, so we regrouped to plan a new strategy.

The odds of finding the suspect were stacked against us due to the darkness, and we were discussing our options when Deputy Dzemyan suddenly shouted, "There he is!"

I looked over my shoulder to see Dzemyan's flashlight beaming down an embankment behind us and directly on the suspect. He had been lying in a briar patch just a few feet away, listening to every word we were saying as we developed a plan to capture him. The fugitive was unable to run any farther. He was completely exhausted and couldn't even walk without some assistance. The elusive poacher had just completed a grueling journey of nearly 12 miles on the run, with no coat, on a cold November day. He had some cuts on his hands and face, and was breathing heavily as we placed him into my vehicle.

The suspect, Clem, told me that he didn't know who put the sack of venison scraps into the bed of his pickup truck, and he just wanted to get rid of them. He went on to say that some "nut" disarmed him, struck him in the face with the butt of his rifle, and threatened to shoot him. He then declared that one of the troopers had fired some shots at him after shouting the command to halt. Clem told me that he continued to run because he had mistaken the trooper for the "nut from Keating."

"Clem, you messed with the wrong man," I told him. "Next time you see him, thank him for his service in the military, and for not dropping you where you stood."

I took Clem to the hospital in Renovo to have his injuries checked and then transported him to the district judge's office. He was later released after posting bond on the charges of possessing parts of a deer in closed season and resisting arrest.

A trial was held some 30 days later, and Clem was found guilty of both charges. He appealed the guilty verdict handed down by the district judge, and a new trial was granted. The appeal was heard on June 15, 1978 by Judge Carson V. Brown, who was the President Judge of the Clinton County Court of Common Pleas. Judge Brown is an avid hunter and sportsman, and I believe this is why he would take such a great interest in all Game Law violations brought before him. He presided over many appeals during my career, and his decisions were always prudent and rational.

Clem hired a good attorney for the appeal. He then tried to convince the judge that someone had put two bags of venison scraps and bones in the bed of his pickup truck as a practical joke. All he was trying to do, he said, was dump the scraps in the woods. He then went on to tell a harrowing tale of being assaulted, running for his life for 12 miles through snow covered forests and hills, being shot at by some unknown person or persons near Sinnemahoning, and finally being run down in a state of total exhaustion. The entire time, he said, he never knew he was being pursued by the law. It wasn't until he heard someone shout, "State game wardens! Keep your hands where we can see them!" that he breathed a sigh of relief. According to Clem, that was when he realized he had been rescued from the "Keating nut-job."

After hearing Clem's defense, Judge Brown immediately found him guilty of possessing parts of a deer in closed season, and he reserved his decision on the resisting arrest charge. During the course of the trial, I had testified that several fresh deer droppings were found in the bed of Clem's pickup truck. I went on to explain that when the carcass of a deer is bounced around while being transported, fecal matter will often exit that carcass. This cast doubt upon Clem's explanation that two bags of scraps were placed in the truck as a joke, and certainly made it appear, at least circumstantially, that the entire carcass of a deer had been transported in the pickup truck at some point. I believe this may have convinced the judge that Clem knew a lot more about the venison scraps then he was telling.

Within one week, the judge filed a six-page memorandum and verdict in favor of the Commonwealth (Game Commission). The judge referred to the episode as "A somewhat bizarre incident that began around 12:30 PM and ended on that same day around 6:30 PM." He then went on to rule that the defendant's flight from the deputy (Ranger), when ordered to stop, brought him within the prohibitions of the Game Law. Clem was found guilty (again) of resisting arrest, paid a substantial fine, a large attorney fee, and had his hunting and trapping privileges revoked for three years. I gave Jake a copy of the court order and we became friends, sharing some good stories over the years.

This was an unusual case for several reasons. One of which was the distance traveled by the suspect while being completely unprepared. Another was his physical condition, which required medical attention at a hospital. And his bogus claim of being "rescued" by the game warden was ridiculous.

However, the following year I was involved in the genuine rescue of an individual whose physical condition required immediate medical attention. A young man who wasn't prepared for the unexpected, and what was about to happen next.

John was an eighteen-year-old young man who had been planning a winter backpacking trip with his friend David, and they finally had the opportunity to go on January 3, 1979. John had no idea that he would come close to meeting his maker during the excursion. They planned a trip spanning eight days, hiking the Black Forest and Susquehannock trails. The Black Forest Trail is a 42-mile loop trail meandering through Potter, Lycoming and Clinton Counties. The Susquehannock Trail System is an 85-mile loop that roams through the big woods of Clinton and Potter Counties.

John and David began their journey on the Black Forest Trail at Trout Run Road in Lycoming County. They briefly considered canceling because the temperature was close to zero, but decided to push on and brave the weather. David had driven a long distance to meet with John, and that played into their decision. And the trip had been canceled before, so John promised David it wouldn't happen again.

Soon after starting the hike, John and David split up. John believed he knew an easier route, and they agreed to meet later in the day where the Black Forest Trail reaches the County Line Branch of Young Woman's Creek. Shortly after they parted ways, John crossed a stream and accidently stepped into a deep spot that was over the top of his boots. Cold water seeped inside and drenched his socks; his feet quickly became numb. John removed his boots and socks, poured the water out of his boots and squeezed as much as he could from his socks. Then he put the wet socks back on and shoved his cold feet back into his boots, and as he continued to walk, he started to regain some feeling in his feet. He didn't want to return to his vehicle because there was no way to contact David.

John pushed on and eventually reached the spot where they were to meet. He was worried at first because David wasn't there yet. And he was cold, very cold. When David arrived and found out what happened, he suggested that they could return home. But John said he wanted to continue with the trail hike they had planned. He didn't want to disappoint David, and thought he could deal with cold feet until they set up camp. Somehow they got off trail and followed the headwaters of Young Woman's Creek for a time, eventually coming upon a hunting camp where they stopped to rest. The thermometer at the camp read five degrees below zero.

After a brief rest, they pushed on. They reached Fork Hill Road and decided to follow it up the mountain rather than risk crossing the stream. Fork Hill Road was covered with a sheet of ice. It is an unmaintained dirt state forest road, considered impassable by anything other than a snowmobile this time of year. The road was so icy and steep that snowmobiles would require steel track studs to be safe. John was carrying a 70-pound backpack and was nearing exhaustion. He was very fatigued by now, but they continued the trek up Fork Hill Road. They were weary, and it seemed to take forever to reach the summit.

They decided to make camp at Rattlesnake Trail, which was close to the Susquehannock Trail system. They set up a two-man tent, started a campfire, and John tried to cook something with his backpack stove. He decided not to wait for food because of the cold. He was shivering, and thought that it would be best to get inside his sleeping bag to warm up. John couldn't stop shivering because hypothermia was setting in. This can occur when the body loses heat faster than it can produce it. The symptoms can include shivering, a weak pulse, confusion, dizziness, and eventually the loss of consciousness. Hypothermia is a medical emergency and immediate medical attention is required. Prolonged untreated hypothermia will result in death.

John was in serious trouble, and he knew it; he couldn't stop shivering. Dave gave him some food and wrapped a space blanket around his sleeping bag. It didn't help. Then Dave boiled some water and put it in a bottle. He placed the bottle inside John's sleeping bag, but to no avail. Dave knew it was time to get help. He had spent a year in the Special Forces in Iceland, and was confident he could do whatever it took to find help. He grabbed his map and some food, and began hiking to the nearest town. North Bend was more than ten miles away. Meanwhile, John was shivering uncontrollably and believed his life would soon end. He knew he couldn't survive until morning.

North Bend

It was late that night when I got a phone call from two emergency medical technicians, Paul James Fantaskey and Jesse Francis. They asked me to help them get to the victim as quickly as possible. They knew what the road conditions were like, and didn't have a vehicle capable of making the trip.

It was very cold, below zero in the valleys and at least 15 below on top when I met them along Young Woman's Creek at North Bend. We hastily attached chains to all four tires of my 4WD patrol vehicle. Fork Hill Road isn't much more than a cow path by most people's standards. This state forest road is the steepest and most formidable in my entire district. It is barely wider than the average car, and there are no guardrails. The road transverses the face of a steep mountain, and slipping off the edge would probably be fatal. The Bureau of Forestry had a sign posted at the bottom that said, "Travel At Your Own Risk," and that was meant for the summer time! The road was covered with snow that had been packed down by snowmobiles, followed by some thawing and refreezing. The result was a solid bed of ice, and I was hoping the weight of my patrol car would press against the chains enough to make them bite through.

We decided the fastest route would be to ride up the right branch of Young Woman's Creek Road to the north entrance of Fork Hill. We made good time, because part of that road is paved and it was clear of ice.

My heart was in my throat when we started up Fork Hill Road that night. It was four long miles to the top, where the victim was lying in a semi-conscious state. I could immediately tell that the chains were biting into the ice as my patrol car slowly crawled up the mountain road. We were very tense. If the vehicle would lose grip and spin out, I couldn't safely back it down the icy mountain. However, I had traveled in conditions like this before, and I believed we could get the victim out.

The icy conditions caused the wheels to briefly spin on the steepest sections, but the chains provided enough grip to get us on top of the mountain. I think the three of us were holding our breath the entire trip. We soon came upon a tent and scrambled over to it, hoping for the best. John was shaking uncontrollably in his down-filled mummy sleeping bag. He was delirious and unable to walk. Paul and Jesse provided emergency medical treatment, and then we lifted him into my patrol vehicle and started down the mountain. The trip down was scary. Going up you have a certain amount of control if the chains are biting. Pressing lightly on the gas pedal causes the 4WD system to distribute power to all four wheels for maximum traction. But going downhill is a different story…all you have is your religion.

I shoved the transfer case shifter into low-range and we all stopped talking. We were tense. The patrol vehicle crept down the icy mountain road barely faster than walking speed. That was the objective, because I didn't want to touch the brakes. In those days, anti-lock brakes were unheard of, and one touch of the brake pedal could have caused the vehicle to go into an uncontrollable slide. I'm thankful that it was such a dark night, because we couldn't see the steep drop-off at the road's edge. Still, I was familiar enough with the road to know it was straight down to the nearest big tree.

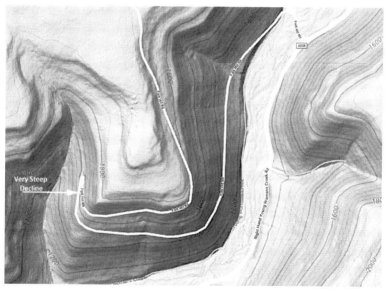

About halfway down, we came upon the steepest part of the road, which approached a 45-degree angle. It was so steep that the weight of my car caused it to travel faster than the 4WD system was capable of holding it back, so the wheels began to slip and spin. Oddly enough, what usually helps is giving it the slightest push on the gas pedal. This will transfer power to the wheels and make the chains bite. I had to do this immediately…before the wheels could spin excessively, causing a loss of control. It is a maneuver that can work under the right circumstances, with an experienced driver who is familiar with these conditions. And it did work. By midnight, we were able to get John safely down the mountain and over to the Renovo Hospital for treatment. John spent two days in the hospital being treated for frostbite, hypothermia and shock. Thankfully, he was able to fully recover.

About 20 years later, I happened to bump into him while I was off duty. John looked good, and we talked about that long night in the dark, deep woods of Clinton County. It was a night that neither he nor I will ever forget.

Nature subjects the weak to the strong.
~Seneca

Dances with Bears

IT WAS MAY 31ˢᵗ 1985 WHEN THE DAY suddenly turned to night like an unexpected solar eclipse. Intense rain transformed into quarter size spheres of hail, hurtling to the ground from an enraged sky. Then came the wind. Softly at first, like an ominous whisper. Mother Nature was about to throw a tantrum!

The ferocity of the wind rapidly increased, giving birth to a gigantic tornado. It was invincible! The force of its savage winds destroyed everything in its path. The sound was deafening, as though a dozen freight trains were passing overhead. The twister cut a 28-mile-long path through the forested mountains of Clinton County, its destructive swath was nearly one mile in width in some places. Trees were snapped like matchsticks from the explosive 150 mph to 200 mph gusts. In all, 15,000 acres of forest and 60 cabins were damaged or destroyed in the Sproul Forest District here. Timber damage alone was over fifteen million dollars.

The destruction in neighboring counties was much worse. Sixty-two people were killed and seven hundred were injured throughout Pennsylvania. President Reagan declared neighboring Lycoming County a disaster area.

East Branch Swamp was directly in the path of the mighty tornado. The swamp forms the headwaters of Big Run, and was designated a Natural Area by the Bureau of Forestry. A large stand of virgin hemlock and white pine embraced the swamp, providing a cooling shade on the hottest of summer days, as the sun couldn't penetrate the massive canopy created by these old trees. They stood as a reminder of what Pennsylvania forests were like prior to the logging era during the late 19th century. East Branch Swamp was not well known. There were no signs pointing to its location; nor were there any picnic tables, park benches or manicured lawns at the entrance of this lonely segment of forest. East Branch Swamp was my place of voluntary exile from the world. It was a place I could go to think. To be alone. To be isolated in the seclusion and privacy of a remnant 19th century wilderness.

Natural progression in nature is often so gradual that it's imperceptible, but at times it can be instantaneous and brutal. And so it was like the death of a good friend when the virgin forest surrounding East Branch Swamp was destroyed by a dispassionate tornado. Not a single tree was left standing.

Light gray area over mountain shows swath of destruction from tornado.

Two weeks after the tornado touched ground, on June 14th 1985, 48-year-old George Kelley of Euclid, Ohio entered the Fish Dam Run Wild Area to go fishing and vanished without a trace. Although he had been there often in the past, he was unaware that a large portion of the area had recently been ravaged by the twister. George parked his car near the headwaters of the run and entered the woods on foot.

The forest surrounding Fish Dam Run seemed perfectly normal at first. But all too suddenly, one would find himself climbing over huge trees scattered haphazardly on the ground. The only way to travel through the blow-down was to walk on top of the fallen timber and step or jump from tree to tree. In some areas, the fallen trees were so close together that George could have been walking on a tree-trunk without realizing he was 10 to 15 feet above the ground. This could be very dangerous. If he would slip and fall through to the ground, the dense foliage would conceal him. If unable to get out by his own power, he would be doomed.

The Bureau of Forestry coordinated an intensive search for Mr. Kelley when he was reported missing. Huge search parties with tracking dogs combed the area. In many sections, the dogs were unable to penetrate the blow-downs, and after seven days, the search was called off. George Kelley was never found.

I didn't participate in the search. However, I did examine Mr. Kelley's parked vehicle in cooperation with the Pennsylvania State Police. When we opened the trunk, I noticed a cardboard bait container tucked away in the corner, the kind often used commercially for worms. I opened the container and there was fresh moist dirt sticking to the bottom and sides. I told the troopers that in my opinion Mr. Kelley emptied that container into something else, possibly a metal bait container commonly worn on the belt when trekking into a forest stream to fish for native trout. It was my opinion that he was, in fact, somewhere in the Fish Dam Run Wild Area.

One of the search teams from outside the area was concerned about the possibility of a bear attack. So before I left the area, I made a trip out to their base camp and explained that they had nothing to fear. I answered a lot of questions, and I was able to eliminate any apprehension that some of the men had about bears.

Bear complaints are a common occurrence in the Northcentral region of Pennsylvania. Like many of my neighboring officers at the time, a good deal of effort was spent trapping and relocating nuisance bears from spring through fall. During the late 1970s, I did a great deal of bear trapping for the Game Commission's bear research program. These were not nuisance bears, and they did not have to be relocated. They were released at the capture site after being processed. Processing would include affixing a metal tag to each ear, removing a tiny premolar tooth, taking body measurements, and sometimes extracting a small amount of blood for various categories of lab work. Occasionally, an inner lip tattoo would be applied as a tracking number identification mark in case the ear tags were lost. Whenever possible, the bear would also be weighed. The bear's age would later be determined by a microscopic examination of the premolar tooth.

The Bitumen Dump was the best place to capture black bears in my district. Environmental regulations eventually shut down the dump. However, it was heavily frequented by bears during its heyday in the 1970s, and I remember seeing as many as 15 different bears foraging for garbage there in a single night. Caravans of automobiles would converge on the dump each evening, portraying a circus-like atmosphere with bears as the entertainment. The garbage would generally be piled 20 feet high, and the bears probed about it while devouring mouthfuls of meat and vegetable scraps.

One night a carload of teenagers drove up from Lock Haven to watch the bears. Most of the people that visited the trash heap were intimidated by the bears, and these kids were no exception. It was late at night, in the middle of the week, and they had the entire show to themselves. At least a half dozen bears were foraging for scraps while the teens excitedly viewed them with a spotlight from the safety of their automobile. After a couple hours passed, the driver attempted to start his car only to discover the spotlight had completely drained his battery. The teens were afraid to leave the safety of their car to get help. They stayed in the vehicle until daybreak before one of them had the courage to run to the nearest home for assistance.

In 1979, Game Commission Biologist Jack Giles and I ran a snare-line for bears at the dump. The snares were made from ¼-inch steel cable, and are used in conjunction with a special spring-loaded triggering device. They are set on the ground in a manner that causes a bear to step into the loop, and when triggered, the spring quickly pulls the snare around the bear's leg just above the paw. These snares are very effective when properly used, and a good set can sometimes take an hour or more to construct. The end of the snare is attached to the base of a tree and is designed to hold a bear without injury.

The area around the dump was so heavily used by bears that well-trodden trails could be found scattered throughout the woods. A long line of staggered paw impressions at least one inch in depth could be found along many of these trails, and in softer ground, the paw indentations would be several inches deep. Each bear using these trails would step into the same series of paw impressions as it approached the trash heap.

We set eight snares on the first day. There was a lot of work involved preparing each trap site and we didn't finish until sunset. The following morning we returned shortly after sunrise and were delighted to see we had captured four bears, all within sight of each other. Before they could be processed, we had to tranquilize them. A nine-foot-long aluminum pole with a special heavy-duty syringe was used to inject a tranquilizing drug into the hindquarter or front shoulder. A black bear is a very docile animal, but under these circumstances some would become aggressive. It can be quite exhilarating to approach within nine feet of a large black bear and poke it in the shoulder with a "jab-stick." I would get a huge adrenalin rush standing near a 500-pound bear that was clacking his jaws, warning me to stay away. Occasionally a bear would lunge toward me just as I injected it with the syringe. Thankfully, in each instance, the snare held it back. The vast majority of bears we snared just sat on their haunches and stared at us.

Black bear caught in foot snare.

All four of the snared bears were males, and after we finished processing them we had to reconstruct each set. The following morning we captured four more bears. Over the course of the summer, Jack and I ended up with a total of fourteen bears at the dump, and an additional nine or ten in other locations of my district.

During the summer of 1980, Jack and I decided to try doing things the easy way. One night we took a ride up to the dump armed with an arsenal of jab-sticks and tranquilizing drugs. Our intention was to drug as many free-roaming bears as we could safely approach. There were at least a dozen bears at the garbage heap when we arrived. It was warm and sticky that night, and several of the bears seemed to be in a feeding frenzy, ravenously gulping down huge mouthfuls of putrid garbage. One large male was acting very aggressive. He would lunge at or charge any bear foolish enough to get too close. We decided to avoid him, at least for the time being, and started with a more well-behaved 200-pounder.

We had decided earlier that Jack would poke the bear with the jab-stick because he was smaller than me and could run faster. We approached the bear with caution, then, with the speed of a lightweight boxer, Jack thrust the jab-stick into the bear's rump. And with the speed of Olympic sprinters, we turned and raced for our vehicle! But the bear hardly even noticed, and when I looked over my shoulder, I could see that he was still gorging himself with food, so we returned for a closer look. We felt pretty brave now, and decided to inject another bear while waiting for the first one to go down from the influence of the drug. The advantage of using the jab-stick was that the bears would not run off, as they often do when smacked by a dart from a tranquilizing gun.

After injecting the second bear, we waited patiently for the drugs to take effect, but nothing happened. After 20 minutes passed, it didn't seem like either bear was going to go under. Something was wrong. We inspected the equipment and noticed that the rod that holds the syringe to the jab-stick was bent, preventing a full dose from entering the bears.

We changed rods and tried it out on a third bear, but the new rod also bent. Another 20 minutes went by, and we were about to pack it in for the night when the first bear we injected walked a few steps toward us and collapsed. The lighter doses were taking effect; it just took more time. The second bear had walked away from the garbage pile, but I could still see him at the edge of the woods. The third bear was between the garbage pile and the second bear, and within a few minutes, they both went down. Since the drug was taking so much time to take effect, we decided to inject a fourth bear. We figured it would be under the influence of the drug by the time we finished processing the other three bears. Unfortunately, we had to walk right out into the middle of the garbage dump to get to him, and the odor emanating from the rotting refuse was enough to blur my vision.

It was just our luck that the drug took effect almost immediately after we poked him with the jab-stick. We were hoping that he would walk out of the garbage before the drug took hold, but he flopped down right in the middle of one of the more putrid sections of the dump.

Jack and I processed the first three bears as quickly as

possible. We then had to trudge through a considerable amount of maggoty, liquefying garbage to reach bear number four. He was a large male weighing in the vicinity of 500 pounds. I made a quick check and could see that he was breathing normally, and that his eyes were open and reacting as they should while under the influence of the drug. I kneeled down and began removing a premolar tooth with my dental extractor when I noticed the ground was infested with wolf spiders! They are quite large and usually solitary. I've always had an aversion to wolf spiders. They caused me to forget about the rancid smell of the bear's bad breath, and the suffocating stench of the steamy garbage on this hot, humid summer night. I quickly looked up at Jack to tell him about the horde of spiders and suddenly noticed that the air was saturated with bats. They were everywhere! There were at least 40 bats circling just over our heads. Apparently the headlights from several cars parked at the dump had attracted an abundance of insects, which in turn drew in the bats. I've always had an aversion to low flying bats, but the bats caused me to forget about the swarm of spiders crawling all over the ground near my feet.

Jack said, "Hey, forget the bats, look behind you!" There, in a semi-circle around us, stood a solemn assemblage of six large bears; their silhouettes only faintly discernible against the dark sky. Our presence in the midst of their smorgasbord seemed to have them confused, so they patiently waited as if curious spectators while we finished our work. I've always had an aversion about being watched while I work. This just wasn't my night.

After we finished wallowing in the garbage with bear number four, Jack and I tranquilized and processed two more large bears. We had done six in all, a good night's work to say the least. We processed every bear that would allow us to approach it without running away. However, there was still one bear remaining. It was the big aggressive boar that wouldn't tolerate other bears in his presence. He was immense. A hulking, bloated, brooding monster. His stomach was so large that it nearly touched the ground. Bears are usually shy creatures, but this brute was an exception. He was mean and ferocious when approached by another bear.

He was at the outer edge of the garbage pile, so we decided that one of us would sit on the hood of Jack's state truck with the jab-stick, while the other operated the vehicle. I suggested to Jack that he should sit on the hood, because he was much smaller and lighter, thereby making it unlikely the hood would be dented.

"Just think about all of the paperwork you'll have to fill out if I buckled the hood of your state vehicle," I reasoned. Jack hated paperwork (I knew this), so he readily agreed to sit on the hood.

I approached the bear very slowly, hoping that he wouldn't be annoyed while gulping down huge chunks of "convenience food." I was able to get within 25 feet of him before he whirled around to face us, clacked his powerful jaws together several times and then made an explosive rush for the truck. A large cloud of dust erupted from beneath his massive paws as he burst forward. The bear came to an abrupt stop just before reaching the truck as Jack scrambled for the roof. At the same time, I began backing away, causing Jack to slide down the windshield onto the hood, so I hit the brakes and Jack slid back and slammed against the windshield. We later agreed to practice this maneuver, with Jack insisting he would drive the next time.

With the fat rippling on his back and his stomach swaying side to side, this irritable, unusually aggressive boar turned and loped back to his private dining area. We decided to return to the dump the next day, only this time we would bring a tranquilizer gun.

The following night, Jack met me in Renovo. He had a biology student with him who was involved in a high school project about the Pennsylvania black bear. After Jack introduced me to the young man, we drove out to the dump and waited for the bears to arrive. We must have spooked the local bear population the night before, because only two rather timid bears made an appearance. They wouldn't let us get close enough with the jab-stick, so we decided to use the gun.

Jack used a syringe to carefully fill a dart with the proper drug dosage for the larger bear. Then he loaded the dart into the rifle and aimed for the bear's rump. When the dart smacked the bruin in the rump, it immediately ran for the woods. We followed after the bear, hoping we would be able to find it. The student seemed very apprehensive about looking for a "wounded" black bear in the woods at night, and the longer we looked, the more nervous he became. After searching for a half hour, it became obvious that we weren't going to find it. The darts were not always reliable. Sometimes the full dose wouldn't be injected, and occasionally they completely malfunctioned and nothing would be injected. However, if the bear had gone down from the drug, the effects would wear off within two hours and the dart would eventually fall out.

I was determined not to let the night become a total loss, and decided to have some fun. There was a large dead bear under a pine tree not too far from where we were standing. We found it two days earlier while scouting for bear trails. There were no external injuries on the carcass, and it most likely ate something toxic to its system.

"Hey Jack," I whispered, "I'll bet I know where we can find the bear."

"Where?"

"I have a hunch he ran over that way," I said, pointing toward the pine tree with a discreet wink. Jack's face beamed with a wide grin and he agreed that we should walk over in that direction. The student was excited by our sudden enthusiasm, and tagged along safely behind us. After walking 75 yards, I stopped and shined my flashlight on the dead bear. "Look! There it is!" I said.

I quickly peeked over my shoulder at the student as he stepped several paces backward. I called him over to me and reassuringly put my arm around his shoulder. Then I asked him to walk up closer to the bear, to make certain it was under the control of the drug.

"Why me?" he asked.

"Because you're the youngest." I whispered.

"Huh?"

"Go on," I urged. "Just walk up within twenty feet of him and toss some pebbles on his head. Don't worry. We're right here. He won't hurt you."

"Are you sure?" he said, his voice trembling a bit.

"I'm absolutely certain this bear can't hurt you."

The student cautiously approached the bear, and after what seemed like an hour, picked up a few stones and tossed them on the dead bear. He hollered back that the bear hadn't moved, so I told him to get closer and throw more stones. The boy would take a few steps and throw a stone, repeating this process over and over until he was within a few feet of the bear.

"Yuck! He's got maggots on him," he screamed. "And he stinks!"

"Must be from an old wound," I shouted as we jogged up to the bear. Jack and I were nearly gagging from the stench as we kneeled down and feigned examining the bear.

"He's dead!" I exclaimed with an expression of shock on my face. We both looked at the student, pretending to be surprised by what we had discovered. Then I looked at Jack and said, "Oh well, looks like we overdosed another one. I guess there's no use hanging around here any longer."

The teenager's jaw dropped. "You mean this happens a lot?"

After a brief pause, we both stood up and started laughing. The student must have thought we were spaced-out from inhaling garbage fumes. After I explained the whole thing was a hoax he started laughing too. On the way back to the truck, he told me he would never forget the night he spent with us at the Bitumen Dump.

It is great cleverness to know how to conceal one's cleverness.
~Francois de La Rochefoucauld

Willy Nilly

I WAS ALONE. There were no lights anywhere. Even the stars were invisible, as those twinkling points of light were concealed by a thick layer of clouds. I was in my patrol vehicle, hidden behind thick brush while I gazed upon an obscure roadway that seemed to be forgotten by civilization. It was a warm, moist mid-summer night back in 1984, and the damp fragrance of the surrounding forest was intoxicating.

I just started to doze off when something gently brushed across my chin. A gypsy moth was attracted by a dim glow coming from my two-way radio, and it began to thrash itself against the control panel. Then it fluttered about in despair, finally deflecting off of the windshield and plopping into my cup of hot black coffee.

Just great! I thought. *My last cup of coffee and it gets polluted by a moth looking for a mate.* I emptied the cup out the window and closed up my thermos. It was time to go home anyway. Hours had passed without seeing a single car. I was on the alert for poachers, deep inside the Sproul State Forest ten miles south of Renovo. I had a good view of State Route 144, a remote paved highway connecting Renovo to Moshannon (population 280). There are no homes, electric lines, or telephone lines along this 25-mile stretch of road within the Sproul.

As I reached for the ignition key, a glint of light caught the corner of my eye. I looked up and saw a spotlight shining way off in the distance. The light was approaching my position, so I stayed put. At the very least, I had a minor spotlighting violation, as it was well past the legal hour ending at midnight.

Perhaps the occupants of the vehicle had guns with them. Spotlighting while in possession of a firearm is a serious violation, and the penalties are quite severe.

If I needed assistance at this late hour, my two-way radio would be useless. The Game Commission dispatcher had gone off the air hours earlier. There were no township police here; the nearest State Police Substation was 40 miles away, and the spotlight was getting closer.

The vehicle finally broke over a hill in front of me. I figured there were at least two people in the car because the spotlight was coming from the passenger side of the automobile. They were headed in my direction, so I decided to wait for them to drive by me. It would be safer to approach them from behind. My heart raced as I considered all the things that could go wrong.

I was in a situation that every game warden has faced before: alone in a remote area at night and about to apprehend some unknown subjects committing a Game Law violation. It is an intense, stimulating experience. It can scare you. Thrill you. Addict you. Why else would anyone take such risks?

After stopping the vehicle, I discovered the occupants were just a couple of 16-year-old kids, a boy and a girl, with no firearms. The boy told me they heard some shooting earlier in the night, a few miles to the east. I gave them a stern warning and sent them home. I was relieved and disappointed at the same time. The adrenalin rush was gone, and I realized that I wanted it to be something more serious: poachers, not children! Perhaps I was addicted to the rush, the danger, and the excitement. It would explain why I was by myself in the middle of nowhere, late at night, with no chance of getting help if things got ugly.

I went home and managed to get a few hours sleep before my phone started ringing. The Renovo Police discovered the carcasses of several deer that were dumped in the borough, and they wanted to meet with me.

The deer remains were located at the west end of town. When I arrived, I inspected the carcasses and found that each deer had been shot in the head, and that only the hindquarters were removed. Unfortunately, I was unable to recover any bullets, as they were all through-and-through wounds. Some people will tolerate the closed season killing of a deer when the entire animal is used. However, killing a deer only for the hindquarters is largely viewed with disgust and contempt. Knowing this, I developed a plan to discover who was responsible for killing these deer.

I contacted Carl Vroman of the local *Renovo Record* newspaper and asked him to photograph the carcasses. I gave him a carefully worded written statement designed to get the attention of the townsfolk, and hopefully infuriate whoever was responsible for killing the deer. I figured that if everybody got upset enough, someone would contact me with relevant information. In the news release, I referred to the outlaws as slobs, and stated that they had left most of the meat behind to spoil. I stated that all three of the deer had been nursing fawns, and "innocent baby deer would surely perish." I purposely used "baby" instead of "fawn" in the news release for a more dramatic effect.

"This is really unfortunate," I stated in the news release, "Because many deer produce twins, we are looking at a potential loss of up to nine deer to this lowlife. And we don't know how many other deer may have been mortally wounded." I went on to state, "The shots were not very well placed, which indicates that this person is not a proficient marksman." Then I asked for anyone with any information to call me, and I included my home phone number in the news release. I hoped that the person who shot the deer would be offended by my comment about his poor shooting ability, and that he would complain to some of his friends about my conclusion. After all, I *was* telling a fib, but for a righteous cause. I had a hunch that the photograph and accompanying news release would produce results.

Since the newspaper was only published on Wednesdays, I had to wait a few days to see if my scheme was going to work. A few days after the paper came out, two individuals made contact with me. They said that Bill "Willy" Nilly was badmouthing me about the news release. Willy was a slob, but he was also a proud slob, and wasn't about to let anyone call him a lousy shot, including me. Unfortunately for Willy, he had no idea how much his actions offended the townsfolk.

I recognized the name immediately, as Willy had a reputation for doing some terrible things. I remember an incident where he was upset with a ruling that a district judge made against him. Willy gathered up a bag full of newspaper and marched right up the steps of his front porch, whereupon he commenced to start a fire. Fortunately, the judge was home and happened to notice Willy hunched down on the deck. The judge was able to put the fire out before the bag became fully engaged.

Weeks later, someone threw a starburst firecracker taped to a rock through the same judge's living room window at three in the morning. The judge and his family were sleeping, but the sound of breaking glass was enough to awaken them. The interior of the home was set on fire but quickly extinguished by family members before any major damage could occur. Willy was the prime suspect but charges were never filed because there were no witnesses.

But this time things would be different. I was able to get enough information from the two informants to secure a search warrant for Willy's home, and was certain I could make a case. After meeting up with Ranger, we drove over to Willy's house to serve the warrant. By coincidence, we arrived there just as Willy and a friend known as "Stretch" were returning to the home.

W illy didn't look very surprised, and I had a feeling that he may have been expecting us. I handed him a copy of the warrant and told him to unlock the front door. I told Stretch that he was not permitted to enter Willy's house until we were finished searching. Stretch wanted to argue about it, so I expressed myself in terms that he would clearly understand.

"Listen," I said. "If you think the last Game Law fine you paid was expensive, wait until you see what it's going to cost if you try walking through that door."

Stretch looked down at the sidewalk for a few seconds, and then he looked up and opened his mouth as if he was about to say something. But he didn't. He turned around, walked back to Willy's car, and sat down inside.

It had only been two years since I arrested Stretch and his friend, Opey Doke for killing a deer in closed season, so he knew I was serious when I warned him about a fine if he didn't back off. The incident occurred near the Bitumen dump on a cool mid-October afternoon. A man was pointing toward a deer for two of his children to see when a shot rang out, dropping it to the ground. All three of them quickly crouched down and watched to see what would happen next. Within moments, they observed a pickup truck creeping along a dirt trail close to where the deer had been standing. Nobody inside the truck made an attempt to retrieve the deer, but the odds were that someone inside that truck shot it. The father was able to get a good look at the truck, and he and his children immed-iately left the area to report it.

As luck would have it, Pop was able to contact me soon afterwards. He gave me a good description of the truck: black in color with a large chrome roll bar in the bed. By the description he provided, I was confident that Opey was responsible for shooting the deer, as I'd seen him driving the same truck around town. I had a hunch that he would be back to get the deer, so after locating the carcass, I concealed my vehicle in the woods and waited patiently for Opey to return.

After an hour passed, I could hear a vehicle driving slowly up the road. I peered out carefully from the bushes and watched as a black pickup truck came to a stop across from the deer. It was Opey. He'd gone to town to pick up Stretch and their two girlfriends. I watched Opey and Stretch drag the deer out of the woods while the girls, acting as lookouts, giggled nervously. After the deer was loaded in the pickup and they were about to drive off, I pulled up behind them and hit my lights and siren. As I was exiting my patrol vehicle, Opey jumped out of his truck, threw his hands into the air and blurted out that he shot the deer; then he puked. Stretch sat there with his head in his hands, and the girls turned white as ghosts. Both of the young men paid stiff fines. The girls were let off with a stern warning.

The incident with Stretch and Opey lingered fresh in my mind as Ranger and I entered Willy's house to begin our search. After checking every room that could have contained a freezer, we found only one. I opened the freezer door, and at first glance it looked like we were going to come up empty-handed. I took everything out piece by piece, and finally found a package of venison that had been shoved way back in a corner. We seized the package as evidence and asked Willy where he had obtained it, but he wasn't talking. Ranger and I left the house after giving Willy a receipt for the venison.

The next day, I contacted one of the informants that provided information about Willy's involvement in killing the three deer. He told me that Willy had been nervous about the attention the incident was getting from the newspaper article. Willy was taking a lot of heat from some of his friends, and he figured it was only a matter of time until the game warden showed up at his door, so he got rid of the venison. The package I found was probably one that he overlooked.

Both informants wanted to remain anonymous, and they would not testify in court. Willy was unstable and unpredictable, so I understood why they refused to testify against him. Without their testimony, I couldn't prove he killed the three deer that were dumped at the end of town. However, I did have one package of venison that Willy held in his possession after the first day of July. This was a violation of the Game Law back in the mid-eighties. It's not the kind of violation game wardens actively pursue, and I never cited anyone in the past for this offense. But it was all I had, and Willy deserved whatever I could throw at him.

I filed a citation against Willy for the amount set by law: one hundred dollars. He pleaded guilty and was granted installment payments to pay off the fine by claiming a financial hardship. A few days later, Willy contacted the Renovo Police and demanded that they arrest me for stealing some money from his house. The police told him they didn't believe his story and refused to file charges. Willy then went to a County District Judge and filed a private complaint against me for theft. He claimed that I took a one hundred dollar bill off of a dresser in his bedroom during the search.

All private complaints for misdemeanors and felonies must be approved by the district attorney before any formal charges are actually brought against an individual. Later that week the investigator for the District Attorney's Office called me, and we agreed to a meeting. It was his duty to check into all of the facts and make a recommendation to the district attorney.

Two days before I was scheduled to meet with the county investigator, I suspected that Willy was in possession of my seven-cell aluminum flashlight. I had reached down behind my car seat for it and it was gone. The last time I removed it from my car was when we searched Willy's house (I always bring a flashlight for checking basements and closets).

The following day, Harry "Hap" Hazzard flagged me down while I was driving through Renovo. What he was about to tell me would change everything.

Hap and Willy were friends, and Willy told him that he was going to "set me up" because I had fined him for the illegal venison. Willy said it would cost me the same amount of money that he had to pay. Hap told me that Willy found my flashlight lying on his couch after we left the house, and that he had no intention of returning it. I thanked Hap for the information, and I asked why he was revealing this to me in light of the fact that he and Willy were friends.

"Cause it ain't right!" he said. "What Willy did, wasting all that meat and all, it just ain't right." Hap went on to say that he didn't like the fact that I was being set up for merely doing my job, and when a man is caught, he should act like a man and face the penalty. I told Hap that while I was very happy he felt that way, his information wouldn't help me unless he was willing to tell it to the district attorney's investigator. I was shocked by his response, especially since I had cited him in the past for a Game Law violation.

"Of course I will!" he assured me. "I told you it ain't right, didn't I?"

The following day, I arranged for a Pennsylvania state trooper to meet with the district attorney's investigator and me. I wanted both of them to hear what Hap had to say. As promised, Hap met us in an alley in Renovo and repeated everything he told me the day before. He also told the investigators that he would be willing to testify against Willy in court. After Hap exited the vehicle, the county investigator told me he was going to advise the district attorney to disapprove Willy's criminal complaint. He said that would have been his recommendation even without Hap's statement.

The state trooper told me that he would file three serious criminal charges against Willy: false swearing in an official matter, false reporting to a police officer, and theft of lost or mislaid property (my flashlight).

Hap Hazzard's willingness to cooperate was amazing considering what had happened between us several years earlier. Hap contacted me by telephone and told me that his wife had accidently placed his hunting license in the washing machine. According to Hap, she washed his hunting coat but forgot to remove the license that was pinned on the back. He stated that the license was in four separate pieces, but it was still legible so he taped it back together. Hap wanted me to look at the license and give my approval for him to continue to use it.

I met Hap the next day while he was hunting small game near Kettle Creek. He handed me his license and asked me if it was okay to continue using it. It was obvious that it had been submerged in water, and like Hap said over the phone, everything was legible. However, his deer harvest tag looked suspicious, as if it had been filled out and erased. Hunters were only permitted to kill one deer per license year.

"It looks like your deer tag was used before," I told him. "I think you threw the whole license in the washing machine to cover it up."

Hap stood there with a surprised expression on his face and said nothing.

"Well...didn't you?" I pressed.

"No way!" He insisted. "Do ya think I'm nuts? If I had, why would I show it to you?"

"Because you're playing a game with me," I said. "You were hoping I'd let you continue to use the license so you could kill another deer."

Hap stared at me for a long moment, his mouth clamped shut. Then, finally, "You're right," he said. "I used it on a deer I killed during the archery season." Hap knew it was unlawful to possess a deer tag while hunting after having placed it on a legal kill. He also knew it was a minor violation, and his admission would result in only a small fine. But I wasn't quite finished with Hap, and decided to play a game of my own.

"After you killed the deer, you went hunting for another one, didn't you?" I said.

"Well if you think I'm gonna admit to that, then you're nuts." he scoffed.

"Hap, you have a local reputation as a deer slayer." I said. Hap smiled but said nothing. "Which is why I directed Ranger to keep an eye on you this past hunting season."

Hap's smile quickly faded into a frown. He knew Ranger's reputation for stealth in the woods.

I pulled a notebook from my shirt pocket. It was blank but Hap didn't know as I looked it over, pretending to read from it. "Ranger recorded the dates and times he observed you hunting during the archery season." I said, glancing up from the notebook.

Now Hap looked very worried.

"Everything is right here: dates, times...everything." I said. "I'll tell you what I'm going to do: I'm going to send your deer tag to the Pennsylvania State Police Crime Lab, so they can determine the date you filled it out."

"They'll do that for you?" Hap asked with a shaky voice.

"Absolutely. I use the Crime Lab a lot. The Lab did a similar examination for me when Ranger was tracking The Cross Fork Commando."

"Ranger could track the Commando!" Now Hap was physically shaking when he spoke.

"I'm going to compare the date written on your tag with the dates in Ranger's notes. Each day you were hunting deer after the kill date on your tag is a separate offense," I told him. "However, if you want to admit it now, I'll give you a break and only charge you for a single day."

"Boy am I dumb!" Hap blurted. "If I hadn't shown you my license you never would have caught me." Hap admitted he was bow hunting for a second deer illegally, and wanted to pay the $200 fine by way of a field acknowledgment. We made arrangements to meet later in the week. After paying the fine, he walked away cursing at himself and kicking at the ground shouting, "Boy am I dumb!" over and over again.

"Maybe so." I muttered under my breath as I watched Hap walk off. Everything I told him had been a bluff, completely made up, and I couldn't help but feel a little sorry for the guy now that he'd volunteered to testify for me.

Hap Hazzard kept his word. When it was time for the preliminary hearing, Hap showed up early, willing and ready to testify before Lock Haven District Judge John Frazier, a tough, no nonsense ex-cop.

Trooper John Keeler of the Pennsylvania State Police was the prosecuting officer. I was very surprised that Trooper Keeler was able to convince Stretch to testify against Willy, too. There was something about Trooper Keeler's demeanor that enabled him to convince a person to see things the right way.

Stretch testified under oath that Willy made up the story about the stolen money. Hap Hazzard testified under oath that it was a revenge plot because Willy wanted to retaliate against me. Willy was represented by a sharp attorney, but the evidence was overwhelming. District Judge Frazier bound everything over to court for a jury trial, but a month before his trial, Willy pleaded guilty on a plea bargain deal to the charge of false swearing. He received a substantial fine, was placed on probation, and ordered to reimburse me for the flashlight.

I was satisfied with the outcome. Because of the false swearing conviction, Willy's credibility in any future court proceeding was destroyed. That was important to me, because I believed we would meet again one day. And we did, when Willy was in the company of Coyotee Boy, but that story has yet to be told.

Nothing gives one person so much advantage over another as to remain always cool and unruffled under all circumstances.
~Thomas Jefferson

BOOGER JOHNSON

I JUMPED OUT OF THE PICKUP TRUCK just as its wheels came to a complete stop. Then my good friend Bunny quickly sped away, knowing it could be several hours until I returned. I entered the woods alone. For the ninth time this week, I would make my way up the same side-hill in an attempt to apprehend Booger Johnson hunting from a baited turkey blind. But this trip promised to be different from the others. Minutes after entering the forest, I could hear someone working a turkey call from the same direction that the blind was located. It had to be him.

Booger was a hostile, vengeful old man, and because of our troubled past, I had a feeling that this might be a setup. I had been checking the blind at least once, and sometimes twice each day, and the long walks were becoming tedious.

Maybe it's me that he's calling to his gun, I thought. I'd had a number of run-ins with Booger Johnson over the years, all of them bad. I could vividly recall the day in a judge's courtroom when he exploded into a frenzied tirade of hatred against me. He sounded like a raving lunatic, blaming me for his son's misdeeds. *This guy is mental,* I thought. *Definitely unstable!*

I couldn't help but think he might have spotted me in the area earlier in the week. That he might not be hunting turkeys after all. That it might be me he wanted in his sights.

I finally reached the trail I was headed for. It followed beside a clear-cut and would eventually take me into a heavily wooded area where the blind was located. I was getting very close now, and it would only be a few minutes until I reached the blind on this unusually warm November afternoon back in 1989.

I was dressed in full camouflage, and extreme caution was in order as I approached the blind. I needed to concentrate now, but instead my mind began to drift back to an incident that happened years ago. Booger Johnson was screaming wildly at me in the courtroom, his eyes bulging out of their sockets as he leaned into my face.

I quickly shook the image out of my head. I could see someone inside the blind, and it was time to make my move...

My confrontations with the Johnsons started three years earlier with Booger's 35-year-old son Slippery Steve, aka Slip. Two men from Maryland happened to be hunting in the wooded hollow behind the Johnson home. It was the opening day of buck season, and they saw Slip shoot and kill a three-point buck shortly after sunrise. After dressing out the deer, Slip returned to his stand and continued to hunt the remainder of the day. This made the two Maryland hunters, Lou and Bill, very angry. The season limit was one deer. They had travelled a long way to hunt here and were not about to allow this flagrant violation to go unreported.

I received a telephone call that evening from Bill, and he explained in detail what had taken place. I knew Slip hunted almost exclusively in that same hollow, and I figured he would probably hunt there again, so I decided to position myself at the mouth of the hollow just before dark the next day.

Ranger and I patrolled together on that second day of buck season and arrived at the hollow just before sunset. Soon after dark, we could see someone in the forest walking toward us holding a flashlight. We stood at the edge of the woods behind Booger's house and waited patiently.

Slip was surprised to see us when he came walking out of the woods with his rifle. However, he had no idea that we knew he had killed a deer the day before. He readily admitted that he'd been deer hunting, thereby unwittingly incriminating himself. I informed Slip that I had two witnesses who saw him kill a buck the morning before, and then watched him return to hunt the rest of the day.

"Them two lousy flatlanders didn't see nuthin'!" he shouted. "And I don't know nuthin' about no three-point buck!"

"When did I tell you it was a three-point buck?" I asked with a warm smile.

Slip stood silently with a blank stare, knowing full well he just slipped up.

I asked him if we could take a look in the shed behind his father's house, as I suspected the buck would be hanging inside. He abruptly refused to give me permission, and since I didn't have a search warrant, I couldn't legally get inside the shed. Mere suspicion is not enough to get a warrant from a judge.

I seized Slip's rifle for evidence and began writing citations for two separate days of hunting deer after killing the legal limit, and another for failure to tag a deer. I told Slip I would return his rifle after the trial.

Slip's trial was scheduled for the middle of January, some six weeks after the violations had occurred. The night before the trial, Bill called me from his home in Maryland to explain that due to a family crisis, he would not be able to travel to Pennsylvania. Bill assured me that if I could get the case rescheduled for another day, he and Lou would testify.

Ranger and I appeared in court the following morning without our witnesses, and therefore we had no case. Slip was there with his father, Booger, and a sharp defense attorney from Lock Haven. I had no choice except to withdraw the citations. However, I told the defense attorney that I would be refiling the charges in the near future when my witnesses were available. I was in an awkward position, and embarrassed that the trial was canceled at the last minute. Because of the unexpected delay in the trial, I told the defense attorney his client could have his rifle returned immediately. I asked the attorney to have Slip meet me in the courtroom so that he could sign the seizure tag for receiving the gun.

I waited in the courtroom with Ranger and Renovo police officer Cannon while the defense attorney talked to his clients. After several minutes passed, Booger and Slip walked into the courtroom followed by their attorney. Suddenly, and without provocation, Booger became enraged. His shrill, earsplitting voice bounced off the walls of the small courtroom as he verbally assaulted me. With the intensity of a man gone berserk, he screamed and shook, accusing me of damaging the rifle while it was in my possession. I was stunned, because he hadn't even looked at it! Then he insisted that I give his son a full box of ammunition with the rifle so he could test it to see how badly I had damaged the barrel. Booger refused to allow his 35-year-old son sign for the rifle. He declared that I had no case against Slip, and that I made up the entire incident. He screamed, he shouted, and he stomped his feet until my ears began ringing.

Then Slip started shouting alongside his father, making one accusation after another against me. I told the defense attorney that he should advise his clients to calm down before things got any worse. The attorney knew the situation was rapidly deteriorating. He managed to persuade Booger and Slip to quiet down and relax, or so it seemed. As soon as I sat down, Booger started shouting again. He began making more accusations as he came toward me. He was pointing and shaking his finger at me, his nostrils flared, eyes wide and wild. Suddenly, like a blindsided smack in the face, he spit on me and quickly turned to leave the room.

I exploded off my chair. In a heartbeat I was on my feet, towering over Booger. At half his age and twice his weight, I could have broken him in two. The defense attorney, astonished by what had just happened, rushed over and escorted Booger and Slip out of the courtroom. Police officer Cannon subsequently filed a charge of harassment against the old man, and a trial was scheduled for the following month.

In return, Booger filed harassment charges against me the following day, claiming I had grabbed his arm and twisted it.

Booger filed a private complaint because the Renovo Police refused to handle the case. After all, one of their own had witnessed the entire event, and it was obvious that Booger was lying. Even though the charge was preposterous, I had no choice except to defend myself in the courtroom.

Both harassment trials were scheduled for the same day, with Lock Haven District Judge John Frazier presiding over each case. On my request, District Attorney Ted McKnight consented to act as the prosecutor against Booger. Ted was usually far too busy to appear for a summary offense at the district judge level. Normally the district attorney doesn't act as prosecutor until a case reaches the appellate court. However, he made an exception here due to the circumstances surrounding this case. Ted is a very clever attorney; a skillful strategist with many years of experience in the courtroom, and I was fortunate to have him in my corner.

Booger was found guilty of harassment for spitting on me. However, the "war" was a long way from being finished, as the next battle was minutes away and would be fought in the same courtroom.

Since Ted was a prosecuting attorney for the Commonwealth, he was legally barred from acting as my defense attorney. Booger's case against me was next, and I was on my own. However, I was confident that I could defend myself in the courtroom without an attorney. This wasn't my first rodeo.

After an attempt by Booger to convince the judge of my guilt, I called Renovo police officer Cannon and Ranger to testify on my behalf. In the end, District Judge Frazier was not persuaded by Booger's perjurious declaration of what had happened that day.

"Not guilty!" he exclaimed, as the thump of his gavel announced the end of the trial.

Later that day, I refiled the unlawful hunting charges against Slippery Steve and the trial was held several weeks later. This time my witnesses from Maryland appeared, and they did an excellent job of testifying. Although Slip was represented by a clever defense attorney, I presented enough evidence to convince district judge John Frazier to find him guilty of all three charges. Afterwards, Slip filed for an appeal of his convictions, and I was beginning to wonder when, if ever, all of this would come to a conclusion.

Eight months passed before Slippery Steve's appeal was heard by Clinton County President Judge Carson V. Brown. Assistant District Attorney Richard Saxton was in his usual fine form that day, and like the judge, he took a keen interest in Game Law appeals. I was elated that after nearly a year had passed, the arduous court appearances with the Johnsons would soon end.

The two witnesses from Maryland once again made the long trip to Clinton County. Ranger and I also testified, informing the court about our encounter with Slip on the second day of deer season. Following our testimony, the defense attorney put Slippery Steve on the stand to testify in his own defense. After swearing to tell the truth, his solemn declaration to the judge was far different from what he stated to me the day of his arrest. Slip declared under oath that his father, Booger had shot and killed the three-point buck after he (Slip) had only wounded it. Slip also stated that on the second day of the buck season he had been returning from target shooting, not hunting, as the "two lying wardens" had testified.

Assistant District Attorney Saxton was anxious to cross-examine Slip, as he made some blunders during his testimony that would seriously impeach his credibility once exposed. Unfortunately, we were out of time. It was 5:00 PM, and the prevailing rule was that summary appeals would be continued if they were not completed by the end of the day. However, due to the extremely tight schedule that the judge was under, we would have to wait until the next closest day that the court was scheduled to hear summary appeals. And because Clinton County only had one Common Pleas Court Judge, we would have to wait four months, until February, to cross-examine the defendant!

When February finally arrived, Slippery Steve was questioned in detail by the assistant district attorney. Because he had four months to prepare for those questions, we didn't damage his credibility that badly.

In his summary, the defense attorney argued there was sufficient reasonable doubt to compel a not guilty verdict by the court. Judge Brown decided to take the matter under advisement and issue a written decision. I knew that this would probably mean a wait of several more months; however, I preferred a written opinion of his decision as opposed to an immediate ruling. An opinion that is expressed in writing leaves no doubt as to the reasoning used in resolving a case.

Due to an extremely heavy caseload, and a long and complicated murder trial requiring that the judge travel outside the county, it would be in excess of one year before the decision was handed down.

I can clearly remember the apprehension I felt as I opened the envelope received from the courthouse that day. It was a well-written six-page decision, and I breathed a sigh of relief upon reading that Slippery Steve had been found guilty of all three charges filed against him: two counts of attempting to kill a second deer, and another for failing to tag the three-point buck he killed.

Just two weeks later, on a mid-October afternoon, I received a tip that Booger's favorite old blind was restored and baited. The structure was located on the side-hill behind Booger's home, and it hadn't been used for many years.

On my first hike to the blind, I found that the ground surrounding it was saturated with wheat and cracked corn. The blind was larger than it had been in the past. It was built out of tree limbs in the shape of a teepee that surrounded two large trees. One of them, an old Hemlock, provided shelter in all but the most severe weather. Inside the blind were two seats made from small piles of flat rocks.

Booger Johnson's turkey blind, front view.

Booger Johnson's turkey blind, rear view.

Two days later, on the first morning of the fall turkey season, I made my next hike to the blind. Upon arriving, I found two squirrel tails lying on the ground, and some fresh candy wrappers and apple peels were inside the blind, but no hunter.

I regretted not checking the blind the day before, as I surely would have apprehended Booger with two squirrels illegally killed through the use of bait. I returned as often as possible, but it seemed that I was always too early or too late. About midway into the week, I found a crow lying on the ground some 20 yards from the blind. It had been killed by a blast from a shotgun only hours before I arrived.

The next day I returned at first light and concealed myself under a hemlock tree a short distance away. I was dressed in full camouflage and remained there, lying in wait, for several hours during a cold, soaking rainfall. When it reached the point that I sensed hypothermia was beginning to set in, I was forced to give up the surveillance. By noon, the rain finally stopped and the sky began to clear, so I made another hike to the blind. However, the journey proved to be fruitless just like all of the others.

The following day, I assisted U.S. Fish and Wildlife Service special agents in serving search warrants for violations of the Endangered Species Act and had to ignore the blind. Some state game wardens are also United States deputy game wardens. Occasionally we are called upon to assist in serving search warrants, arrest warrants, questioning suspects, conducting field investigations, etc. On this particular day, we seized a truckload of federally protected mounted wild animal specimens from a wildlife museum.

A sudden series of yelps from a hunter's turkey call quickly brought me back to reality. I had been so deep in thought about everything leading up to this moment that I'd lost track of time, and Booger's blind was just ahead. I had to be very careful now. There was a small, dense stand of sapling hemlocks just ahead of me. I planned my approach so that I would be concealed and protected by those trees. As soon as I stepped around them, I would be exposed to anyone inside the blind, perhaps only 30 yards away at best. Although dressed in camouflage, I would be out in the open and clearly visible. More people are shot in mistake for a turkey than any other wild animal; however, I felt that the risk here was very low.

There was no way I would be mistaken for a turkey, or so I hoped.

My pulse surged as I stepped out from behind the protective shield of shaded hemlocks into the brightly lit clearing. My eyes had to adjust to the sunlight, and time seemed to stand still as I strained to determine precisely where the hunter was located inside the blind. The blind was very large, with its opening entrance directly in front of me, but it was well shaded by the huge hemlock tree it was built around.

I had approached from behind, and gradually visualized the indistinct silhouette of a man standing inside. I continued to peer into the dimly lit fortress, my eyes riveted upon the obscure outline of a hunter that I knew was watching me with equal intensity. My vision finally began to adjust to the shadowed interior of the blind. It was Booger! He was dressed in full camouflage, leaning against the hemlock tree and staring at me.

He didn't recognize me. He was standing there with a sheepish grin on his face, thinking I was just another hunter who had inadvertently discovered his blind. Booger's jaw dropped open when I pulled a badge from my pocket and identified myself. I told him to step out of the blind with his hands behind his head as he gawked at me in utter disbelief.

After seizing his rifle, turkey call, and a small bag of wheat from his jacket pocket, I told him he was in violation of the Game Law. There was no argument this time. Booger walked home and returned one hour later with $400 in cash to pay his fine for two counts of hunting through the use of bait. I handed him an official receipt, and as a result, his hunting and trapping privileges were revoked for the next two years.

Booger Johnson passed away one year and eleven months later.

If a man will begin with certainties, he shall end in doubts; but if he will be content to begin with doubts, he shall end in certainties.
~Francis Bacon

Chasing Poachers

RANGER LEANED OUT THE WINDOW of my patrol car and expelled what seemed like a pint of tobacco juice from his mouth. The brown liquid sprayed the night air and splattered across the dense stand of mountain laurel concealing us.

"We've only seen three cars in three hours, so why don't we pack in?" he grumbled. It was 3:00 AM on a Sunday morning, and we were parked on a trail adjacent to State Route 144, locally known as the Ridge Road. One can travel this road from Renovo toward Moshannon, for a distance of some 25 miles, without encountering any sign of civilization except an occasional hunting camp.

"I hope you're not getting any of that on my door!" I cautioned. "The last time you rode with me I spent an hour cleaning it off the car."

Ranger laughed and told me that was because I'd been driving too fast, making it impossible for him to spit without spraying the car. He offered to use a paper cup instead of spitting out the window, but the thought of driving along a bumpy forestry road with Ranger holding a cupful of tobacco juice in his hand seemed implausible at best. So I suggested that he try chewing raisins instead.

"After all," I reasoned, "you could still spit large quantities of brown juice, and at the same time benefit from the nourishment raisins would provide."

Suddenly we heard a motor vehicle approaching from the head of the Fish Dam Run Wild Area just north of us. There was a full moon that night, and visibility was excellent, but we were well hidden by the dense mountain laurel embracing my patrol car. Soon we could see the bouncing glow of headlights through the laurel. I remarked to Ranger that the car seemed to be traveling much slower than one would expect for this remote but well maintained roadway. When the vehicle was directly across from our location it stopped and the engine and headlights were cut off. Although it was only 50 yards away, the dense laurel made it impossible for us to see what was happening.

Soon we heard the distinct metallic click of the vehicle's door being quietly closed. Ranger was leaning his head out the window, listening for anything that might reveal what they were up to when he jerked his head back inside the car.

"They just shot at a deer!" he hissed.

"What are you talking about?" I said in disbelief. "I didn't hear anything!"

"I'm telling you, they just shot at a deer!" insisted Ranger. I could hear an arrow glancing off of the laurel behind us."

"That's not even possible."

"What's not possible?"

"That you or anyone else could hear an arrow flying through the air."

"I told you, it glanced off some laurel!"

"Okay, if you say so. But what are the odds that anyone would pick a spot 50 yards from two game wardens to poach a deer?"

"Now that's something we can agree on," grumbled Ranger.

"There are a million places someone could shoot at a deer in this remote county at three o'clock in the morning," I said. "Nobody could be this unlucky!"

Suddenly a burst of light beamed out from the mysterious vehicle, and a powerful spotlight scanned the forest behind us. Then, seconds later, the spotlight was turned off and the vehicle started up and began to slowly drive away. The legal time for spotlighting had long been over, which gave me a legitimate reason to stop the car. I waited until it moved down the road a short distance so I didn't give up our hiding spot before making my move.

When I pulled onto the Ridge Road, my headlights illuminated the suspect's vehicle, a 1976 Dodge Charger. There were two men inside; one of them was sitting in the back seat. Then, as I tried to get closer, the driver began to increase speed, and the faster I went, the faster he went. The Charger was too far away to get a license number, and I could see that the driver wasn't going to let me catch up. I turned on my rotating red light, but that only caused him to go faster. The taillights quickly became faint embers of light as the car exceeded 100 miles per hour on the narrow roadway ahead of us.

The suspects were headed toward State Game Warden Jack Weaver's district in Centre County. I told Ranger to try to contact him by radio as I raced down the remote roadway while clenching the steering wheel with both hands. Ranger mumbled something about having to spit first, and before I could react, his head was out the window.

"Darn wind!" he remarked as he pulled his head back inside and reached for the microphone.

"You should have warned me; I would have slowed down," I said with a feigned tone of disgust in my voice.

"Then we would have lost them!" Ranger countered.

"We already have!"

Ranger made contact with State Game Warden Weaver; he told us he'd position himself on the Ridge Road just outside of Moshannon and wait for the Dodge Charger to show up.

"What the heck is that rattling sound I keep hearing?" Ranger asked as I raced down the uneven back road.

"It's one of the bullets we recovered from the three deer Coyotee Boy shot and dumped behind the bar. It's in my ashtray."

"Well, it's kind of annoying," grunted Ranger.

"Yep, and it's staying there until we catch him."

"Seriously?" he said.

I glanced at Ranger then back to the road. "It's a constant reminder that he's out there somewhere poaching deer. It bugs me too, but it's staying there until we get him."

Within minutes, Game Warden Weaver informed us that he was in position several miles ahead of us. At this point, we weren't even sure that the suspects were still on the Ridge Road, as there were several dirt roads scattered along the highway that they could have used to escape.

Suddenly my two-way radio crackled with Weaver's excited voice. "They just got around me!" he shouted. Jack immediately gave chase, while some deputy game wardens that had been listening on the radio headed in his direction. The Dodge turned onto a back road with Jack in close pursuit, but his patrol car was no match for the Charger, and he quickly lost sight of it.

Then, without warning, a pair of headlights began approaching in front of him at a high rate of speed. Jack had a strong suspicion that the suspects had turned around, so he stopped his car in the center of the road and quickly exited. He was in full uniform while signaling for the vehicle to stop as it sped toward him. At the last moment, the Dodge swerved off the road and up an embankment along the woods. Debris scattered everywhere as the vehicle's tires began spinning, tearing out clumps of brush as it chewed its way back to the road. Sparks flew from the impact of the car as it thrust itself back onto the macadam roadway. Smoke poured from the spinning tires as the Dodge sped away, its rear end fishtailing from side to side as the driver tried to control the awesome horsepower of his outrageous machine. Jack quickly jumped back into his patrol car in pursuit of the suspects. He stayed in touch by two-way radio, so we headed in his direction along with two Centre County deputy units that were nearby.

After receiving a radio message from Jack that the Dodge Charger disappeared in the vicinity of the Snowshoe Restaurant and Truck Stop, we quickly proceeded to that location. Jack was there along with some of his deputies, and we began to search the large parking area for both suspects.

Within minutes, we found the Dodge sitting in an obscure section of the parking lot bordering the forest. We cautiously approached the car, expecting a confrontation at any moment, but soon discovered that it had been abandoned. By now we were eight officers strong, so we spread out and entered the woods in search of the two runaways. After a few steps into the trees, I found aluminum hunting arrows scattered everywhere. All together I gathered up 40 arrows and a spotlight that had been left behind while they attempted to escape on foot.

Suddenly, I heard Ranger shout, "Stand up and put your hands behind your head!" Two men, brothers in their late twenties, were crouched behind a large oak tree less than 100 yards into the forest. We marched them out of the woods, and upon questioning, I learned they had attempted to kill a deer. The whitetail was standing within 25 yards of my patrol car when Charlie Hottfoote, the younger of the two, shot at it with his bow. Jimmy Hottfoote, who had been driving at the time, shined a spotlight on the deer as it ran away. Jimmy told me that he threw two brand new Jennings compound bows out the window during the chase. Then he admitted he was so nervous after getting past Game Warden Weaver for the second time, he and Charlie changed positions without stopping the car. He estimated they were doing 90 miles per hour when they made the switch! Both of the men ended up paying substantial fines and had their hunting and trapping privileges revoked. The compound bows were never recovered.

The odds were in favor of Charlie and Jimmy Hottfoote to an extraordinary degree that fateful night. They were deep inside a 500-square-mile section of state forest with no homes, phones, or electricity. I'm sure they believed there was no chance anyone would be watching them, let alone two state game wardens.

I had a similar case back in 1986 involving two young men from Renovo who shot a deer during closed season. They were along an isolated dirt road, and had no idea they'd been photographed by two witnesses.

I received a telephone call late one spring night from a man and woman who observed two suspicious individuals in a remote section of state forest. The witnesses were camping in the woods not far from the road when they heard the thunderous crack of a high-powered rifle. It was early in the evening, and the shot sounded like it had been fired from the dirt road below them. The campers walked out to the road and saw an unoccupied car parked along the edge of the woods. The woman had a camera with her, so she photographed the back of the automobile from a distance close enough to clearly read the license plate number.

Suddenly they noticed two individuals in the woods ahead of them. The woman walked a short distance into the forest and hid in the laurel, while her husband hid behind a tree. Within minutes, the first suspect walked out to the car carrying a bulging plastic bag and a rifle case. He put everything into the trunk and then called to his accomplice, advising him to hurry up before someone came by. Soon the second man walked out to the car carrying another bulging plastic bag. The woman managed to photograph him just before he placed it into the trunk. After the two men got into the car and drove away, the witnesses cautiously investigated the scene. They discovered and photographed the remains of a doe lying in the brush with only its backstraps and hindquarters removed.

Ranger and I met them later that night and they gave us the roll of undeveloped film. Then they took us to the carcass of the deer. The man and woman were very disturbed that the poachers only removed part of the deer, wasting many pounds of venison. They became even more upset when Ranger reached down and removed a fully developed unborn fawn lying in the entrails of the old doe. We assured them that we would do everything in our power to apprehend the people responsible, and thanked them for bringing the matter to our attention.

The following morning, I took the film to a photo processing lab in Lock Haven and had it developed while I waited. The finished photographs of the deer and the car were very sharp, and I could easily read the license plate number. However, the photograph of the second suspect caught him from a side view with his head turned away, and the image was far too small to be helpful. I asked the lab technician to enlarge the image to a poster-print size. I would have to wait 24 hours to see the finished product, and I doubted that I'd be able to identify the suspect from the blown up print. But it was worth trying.

I called in the license plate number and learned that the car was registered to a Renovo man by the name of Leech. I did not know Leech personally, however I knew that he and my old foe Willy Nilly were good friends, and like Willy, he had a reputation of being a little bit crazy.

My next stop was to see District Judge Thomas Bossert for a search warrant. Tom is a former schoolteacher and possesses that rare commodity called common sense. I don't think I have ever walked out of his courtroom without learning something. Tom always managed to blend his teaching profession with his position as a judge when presiding over a trial. After securing the search warrant, I met with Ranger and we discussed the manner in which it would be served.

We arrived at Leech's home shortly before 5:00 PM that evening. I rapped loudly on the door and waited for a response. I didn't know what to expect from Leech or anyone else that might be in the house. However one thing was certain, once the door opened, no one was going to prevent us from entering the home. And if there was no response to my knock within a reasonable amount of time, we were prepared to enter by force.

The door abruptly opened and I quickly placed my foot just inside the opening so it wouldn't be slammed shut. Leech looked stunned as I identified myself and handed him a copy of the warrant. He just stood there with his mouth open and never said a word.

I motioned for him to step aside and we entered the house. Leech's wife was standing near the kitchen holding a newborn baby. She was shocked by what was happening. Just 15 minutes earlier she had returned home from a three-day trip to Philadelphia, and had no idea her husband was involved in the illegal killing of a deer. Because we had a search warrant, Leech readily admitted his involvement in the violation and walked over to the freezer.

"No need to search," he offered, "the meat is right in here." He opened the door and removed ten packages of partially frozen venison. Since Leech was being so cooperative, I asked him to show me the rifle he used to kill the deer. We followed him into the living room and he pointed to a .30-30 Winchester leaning against the wall.

"There it is," he said with a cocky grin.

"Well it belongs to the Commonwealth now," I said as I removed it from its resting place. Leech's grin instantly dissolved as he sat down on a nearby couch. I asked him who his accomplice was, but as I expected, he refused to tell me. I handed him the photographs of the deer carcass and his automobile, and watched him shake his head in disbelief as he examined them. Then I told Leech I had a photograph of his friend, and that it was in the process of being enlarged into a poster size print in order to identify him.

"By tomorrow, I'm going to know who he is," I said. "Why not make it easier on both of you and tell me his name?"

"What do you mean by easier?" he asked.

I looked over at his wife and our eyes met. Then I slowly looked down to the baby she was holding by her waist.

"The doe you killed was pregnant," I said, turning back to Leech. "It had a fully developed fetus, so you could be charged with killing two deer just as easily as one."

"Pregnant!" his wife shouted. "You shot a pregnant deer! You better tell him who was with you, right now!"

Leech turned ghost white as he leaned forward and placed his head in his hands. "I can't squeal on a buddy," he groaned. "It just ain't right."

I explained that he didn't actually have to, and suggested that he go over to his friend's house and show him the photographs as an offer of proof that the two of them were observed at the scene of the violation.

"Tell your friend that the smart thing to do is to cooperate and turn himself in, because his identity won't be a secret much longer," I said. Then added, "And when you bring him back, make sure he comes with his share of the venison."

Leech left the house in his automobile and returned minutes later with a young man that I had arrested in the past for poaching deer. After entering the house together, his buddy, Slinky, handed me a sack full of venison.

"Leech told me you have a poster-sized photograph of me," he said. "So I guess you got me dead to rights."

"That's right," I agreed. "The photo is at the lab now."

Both men pleaded guilty and paid heavy fines in addition to having their hunting and trapping privileges revoked.

The following morning, I drove out to the photo lab in Lock Haven to pick up the poster-sized print. Even though I no longer needed it, I was curious to see how it turned out. The lab technician handed me the enlargement and commented that it was a sharp, well-focused image, but it probably wouldn't be of much help.

"Sure is a great shot of the back of a man's head," I said. "But you're wrong about it not being much help."

Driving back to Renovo, I couldn't help but chuckle as I thought of an old saying that would apply to Slinky: "The problem with some folks isn't what they don't know, but that they know so much that ain't so."

Ethical behavior is doing the right thing when no one else is watching - even if doing the wrong thing is legal.
      ~Aldo Leopold

GREED

IT WAS AN UNUSUALLY WARM NIGHT for the last day of October, and a brilliant moon beckoned John and Linda to take a stroll down to the riverbank. This could be their last chance until spring to walk under a shimmering full moon, its reflection so bright that the river sparkled under its glow. It was a night mild enough for short sleeves as they walked out of the house hand-in-hand toward the river's edge. They stopped and gazed at the moon for a while, then John pointed to other heavenly bodies light years away, yet seemed so near.

"Let's stay here awhile," said Linda as she gave John's hand a gentle tug and sat by a tree. John quickly agreed, and they talked about their future together while admiring the moonlight dancing upon the river.

Tommy Trouble was at home alone that night. He was a 15-year-old boy who lived several houses downriver from John. The archery season had ended the day before, but Tommy decided that tonight would be his chance to kill a deer. He reached up and took his father's compound bow from its shelf, admiring its beautiful design and the power he knew it possessed. Tommy took a razor-sharp broadhead arrow from the quiver and knocked it to the bowstring as he walked out the back door. He knew there were always a few deer near the riverbank, and the moon was so bright that he wouldn't need a light to find one.

Tommy quietly made his way to his neighbor's home along the riverbank hoping to ambush an unsuspecting deer while it was feeding. Like a thief in the night, he crawled along the side of their house until he reached the front corner and peered out across the lawn. He saw two deer a mere 15 yards away and he slowly began to stand for a shot, but the deer dashed around to the other side of the house. Tommy turned and ran to the back of the house and looked, but the deer were nowhere in sight. Thinking they headed a short distance up river to the next neighbor's yard, he carefully stalked them. Ever so slowly, he made his way to a grassy field where Tommy was certain he would find his quarry.

John and Linda were sitting side-by-side, their backs against a large oak tree, when off in the distance came the haunting wail of a screech owl.

Linda grabbed John's hand and squeezed tight. "What was that!" she gasped.

"Just an old hoot owl," said John.

Again it came: a shrill, descending whinny, reverberating through the night.

Linda squeezed his hand again, harder this time. "It sounds like someone screaming for her life!" she hissed. "I'm scared, John."

Tommy was standing at the edge of the grassy field, straining to catch sight of the deer that ran off. Dozens of trees were scattered throughout the clearing, their shadows making it difficult to see. Suddenly, he noticed something under the cover of a large oak just ahead.

John and Linda never saw Tommy; they were too focused on the owl. Linda was shaking with fear and wanted to run home. She started to get up, pulling John's hand, but he was being stubborn.

Tommy zeroed in on the movement. A deer! Had to be! He grasped the bow tightly in his left hand and extended his arm, then slowly pulled the bowstring back with his fingertips. The aluminum arrow slid along its rest as Tommy's arm trembled under the tension of the powerful bow. When the cams on each limb finally turned over, the pressure eased, and Tommy took careful aim. The bow was steady now, its razor-sharp broadhead pointed directly at Linda's torso. Tommy unwittingly held her life in his hands as he prepared to release the four-bladed arrow. A bead of sweat ran down his forehead and trickled into his right eye, causing him to flinch as he let the bowstring roll off his fingertips.

An earsplitting scream shattered the night as the arrow brushed past Linda and bored through John's leg, severing muscle and tendons.

"John, what happened?" cried Linda.

John couldn't answer. He instinctively grabbed the arrow and yanked it out. Linda screamed when she saw the blood gushing from his leg. John started to go into shock. He struggled to stay conscious, knowing his fate rested on his ability to get to a hospital as quickly as possible. John knew that if his femoral artery had been cut, he would bleed to death in minutes.

Tommy suddenly realized what he had done, and ran over to the horror-stricken couple. With Tommy's help, John managed to hobble to his car and had Linda drive him to the hospital. Fortunately, the Bucktail Medical Center was only minutes away, and the emergency room physician was able to stop the bleeding in time. John survived the accidental shooting, and eventually regained full use of his injured leg.

I charged Tommy with hunting deer during closed season and shooting a human in mistake for a wild animal. He was fined, placed on probation, and had his hunting and trapping privileges revoked for several years. This was without a doubt, the most bizarre hunting accident I investigated during my thirty-four year career with the Pennsylvania Game Commission.

Over the years, the archery season has often provided me with the opportunity to investigate unusual incidents. I recall one particular case that took place many years ago when I apprehended my old nemesis, One-Eye. It was just before sunset, when I backed my patrol car behind a stand of Norway spruce trees along the Hyner Mountain Road. I planned to remain there until well after dark, as deer could often be found feeding near the roadway at this location. I was boxed into a narrow valley surrounded by steep side-hills.

A narrow, winding roadway traveled up the mountainside directly across from my location. It was a somewhat hazardous route that served as an access road to Hyner View State Park. I wasn't there long when I heard a car descending the mountain roadway at a high rate of speed. Its tires squealed at each curve, and its muffler let out a thunderous rumble that echoed from mountainside to mountainside. At first, I couldn't imagine why someone would race down such a dangerous roadway. The driver was obviously in a hurry and must have felt that the risk was worth taking.

I began to contemplate the reasons why, and had a wild hunch that whoever was driving the car may have killed a deer and left it in the woods. I figured he might have been racing home to borrow a deer tag in case he was stopped by a game warden while transporting the carcass back home. This is how your mind works when you've investigated thousands of Game Law violations over the years.

These sort of crazy hunches rarely pan out, I thought as the car came to the bottom of the mountain and turned onto the road I was watching. All I could see was headlights as the vehicle sped by me toward the village of Hyner.

Fifteen minutes later, a car with a loud muffler came racing up the road from Hyner toward my position. No other vehicles had been by, and I was pretty sure this was the same car that passed by me earlier. The driver turned onto View road and raced toward the top of the mountain. Now I was certain, so I drove over to the bottom of View road and waited. After 30 minutes without a single vehicle descending the mountain, I began having serious doubts about my wild hunch.

Pretty far-fetched, I muttered to myself. *There are plenty of explanations for what had happened.* I was just about convinced I was wasting my time when I heard a car with a loud muffler coming down the mountainside at a leisurely rate of speed. Certain it was the same car, my pulse quickened as I put on my Stetson hat. This "game" I was playing was about to come to a conclusion, and the thrill was far beyond the exhilaration felt in any game bound by rules of fair play.

I will often begin an investigation as though it's a game, albeit a potentially dangerous one. Most people that violate the Game Law are not hardened criminals. Many are hardworking middle-class people that may commit a violation for a variety of reasons. A game warden is like a referee that enforces the rules and regulations of a sport by issuing warnings, or levying penalties. However, all the players in this game carry a gun, and as is true with any sporting event, tempers can flare. Thus, an ever-present element of danger shadows every state game warden.

Game wardens are at a great disadvantage when they approach someone holding a rifle or shotgun while their handgun is snapped securely in its holster. But since the vast majority of hunters are decent, law-abiding citizens, we accept the risk. After all, it would be unreasonable to draw a handgun whenever we approach a hunter. We accept the disadvantage, but remain on high alert.

The suspect's vehicle was about to round a curve just above me, bringing my patrol car clearly into view. I quickly turned on my rotating red light and stepped back into the woods. When the suspect pulled up to my rear bumper and stopped, I stepped out to the road and identified myself. There were three occupants in the car. One-Eye was the driver, his teenage son was sitting beside him, and his 12-year-old daughter was in the back seat. Everyone was decked out in camouflage, and there were three bows stacked together next to the girl.

"Any luck?" I asked.

"Yeah, my daughter got one," One-Eye replied.

When I asked if I could take a look at the deer, One-Eye agreed to open the trunk, but not before going into a lengthy sermon on why he and his family would never violate the Game Law.

When I opened the trunk, there was a large doe inside with his daughter's big game tag attached to its ear. One-Eye told me all three of them were together when she killed the deer up on top of the mountain. He said that after they removed the entrails, he and his son dragged it to the car and loaded it into the trunk.

"Now quit harassing us and let us go home!" complained One-Eye.

"Sure. You can leave," I said. "But I'm real curious about why you made such a hasty trip down the mountain and back not too long ago?"

One-Eye was shocked by my question, and momentarily at a loss for words. After considerable thought, he told me that his daughter forgot her license and he had to go home to get it. One-Eye had a big toothless grin on his face as he stood there bobbing his head up and down in apparent agreement with his explanation. Meanwhile, I also had a grin on my face as I shook my head from side to side. "Wrong answer," I told him.

One-Eye frowned. He didn't expect that type of response from me, and didn't know what to say. But he quickly recovered and started bobbing his head once again. "Then you tell me why I made the trip," he said with a cocky grin.

"I know exactly why. You went home to pick up your daughter and her license so you could put her tag on a deer you killed."

I didn't want One-Eye to suspect that I was just guessing, so I told him that I had been concealed at the edge of the road earlier, and could see that his daughter was not in the car when he drove down the mountain, but that she was when he made the trip back up. It's called "trickery," a legitimate tactic often used by law enforcement officers to game suspects into an admission of guilt.

One-Eye displayed his toothless grin once more and started bobbing his head up and down. He didn't say anything. He just kept grinning and bobbing like some silly department store bobblehead doll.

Come on One-Eye, say something! I thought. Then, finally, after what seemed like forever, he began to speak.

"Well, I guess you got me," he admitted. "But I'll bet I would've fooled you if you weren't hiding in them woods spying on me the whole time."

"Only fools get fooled," I replied. And at that moment, I couldn't help but think that the term *game warden* had taken on a double meaning with the bluff I played on One-Eye.

The common eye sees only the outside of things, and judges by that, but the seeing eye pierces through and reads the heart and the soul.
~Mark Twain

CHEAT SHOT

"**H**EY JOHN, COME LOOK AT THIS!" Deputy Bob McConnell's eyes were wide open, his gray hair lifting fiercely in the wind as he waved me over to the corn feeder. It was the second day of the 1983 bear season, and Bob's discovery would enable me to file some serious charges against two members of Camp Chug-A-Lug. I didn't realize it at the time, but the most complex and demanding case of my career was rapidly unfolding in front of me. Before the matter reached a final conclusion, I would spend more than 60 hours on the investigation, including written documentation and court appearances.

Bear season that year began much the same as so many before. On Sunday, the day prior to the Monday opener, my brother Bill arrived at my home. He drove up from Montgomery County with two deputies and long-time friends Darrel Allspach and Bob McConnell. In those days, we were known as district game protectors, and I jokingly referred to Bill as the "Metro DGP" due to his heavily populated district. However, Bill was quick to remind me that we both grew up in neighboring Bucks County.

"That's right Bill," I said, "but it was rural back in the good ol' sixties."

Bill gave an approving nod of his head and smiled. It was during that time that we developed a great love of the outdoors. Our winters were spent on the trapline, and during the summer months we would spend most of our time camping and fishing. We were inseparable. Bill and I eventually became deputy game protectors in northern Bucks County under the tutelage of District Game Protector Bill Lockett. A few years later, in 1976, we graduated from the 16th class of the Pennsylvania Game Commission's training school located near Brockway.

Bear season was the only time that my brother and I had the opportunity to patrol together. There were no bears in Montgomery County, so Bill would come up to my district with one or two deputies and assist me for several days. Clinton County received tremendous hunting pressure during bear season, and I would always welcome the help.

The opening day found the four of us out on the road before sunrise. We checked several successful hunters in the field before noon, and then decided to visit the bear check station at the forestry office in Shintown.

Shortly after we arrived, Ray "Rainy" Day and Brian Brainfreez pulled in with a large bear in the bed of Rainy's pickup truck. Brian told us he killed the bear early that morning, a few miles from their camp, and that Rainy had been hunting with him. The bear was dressed out, and I estimated its live weight at about 400 pounds.

Because Rainy had killed a bear in the same vicinity the year before, I thought it was odd that he'd be involved with a successful bear hunt two years in a row. I rarely saw him in the woods, and when I did, it was usually during deer season while cruising the forestry roads in his red pickup truck. Rainy was a road hunter, and he didn't possess enough woods savvy to be so successful with the elusive black bear. The annual harvest in those days was nothing like today. In 1982, the statewide kill was only 588 bears, compared to 4,653 in 2019. Statistically, it would be unusual for anyone to participate in a successful bear hunt for two consecutive years.

The next day, we visited their camp to see if it was baited with corn, an all too common practice among some camps prior to bear season. Bears love corn, and once they locate a source they will make regular visits, often using the same trail each time. It then becomes a simple task to position yourself along the trail and ambush an unsuspecting bear. As a matter of fact, if it's done "right" the so-called hunter doesn't have to leave the comfort of his own cabin.

We arrived at Camp Chug-a-lug late that afternoon and observed a large wooden feeder filled with ears of corn directly across from the cabin. Bear droppings were scattered around the feeder, and it was apparent they were frequenting this location as recently as last night. Suspecting that Brian Brainfreez had killed his bear here, we decided to search the area. Because bears shot along a trail leading to bait are often killed some distance away in order to eliminate incriminating evidence, the four of us spread out to explore the surrounding forest. After a thorough search, we were unable to find any sign that a bear had been killed.

Later that evening, when we returned to my home, there was an anonymous message on my telephone answering machine. The caller stated that Brian Brainfreez shot a bear Sunday, the day before bear season, and the entrails were buried in the woods near his camp. We returned to Camp Chug-a-lug the following day around noon to talk to Brian. It was a mild, sunny day with temperatures in the mid-fifties. Brian's bear was hanging from a game pole in direct sunlight and had not been skinned.

I knocked on the front door but there was no answer, so I went around back and knocked on the basement door. Again, no answer, and it appeared that the camp was empty. As we stood there talking, Bill looked down and noticed a single droplet of blood on a stone about ten feet from the door. If the anonymous caller was right, the bear may have been dressed out in the basement. It would then make sense for the entrails to be transported to the woods in a sack of some sort. And if the sack had a tiny hole in it…

The four of us fanned out and closely examined the ground behind the camp. Soon a second droplet of blood was found. Then another. And another! The trail seemed to end at the edge of the woods, but we knew better. A single droplet of blood on a dead leaf can be lost forever with a brief gust of wind. We were down on our hands and knees, scavenging for more signs of blood, when Bob hollered that he found another droplet. The "game" was off to an intriguing beginning, and I was certain many more players would become involved.

While we continued our search, Rainy's truck pulled into the camp yard and parked in front of the bear carcass. I walked away from the search and approached them just as Brian and Rainy were getting out of the truck. Needless to say, they were surprised to see a team of game wardens searching their property.

I asked Brian if he would mind answering some questions. He nodded affirmatively, and we both got into my patrol car. I began to question him about the bear just as Bill stepped out of the woods and walked toward us. His slight, reassuring grin told me they found the gut pile, so I got out of the car and met him halfway while Brian cooled his heels in the passenger seat. Bill told me they followed the blood trail directly to the entrails, which were buried under a large pile of leaves. Bill also cut open the stomach and said it was filled with corn.

We both walked back to my patrol car and I asked Brian where he killed the bear. He said he shot it about three miles from the camp after Rainy dropped him off along a forestry road. He went on to say that after walking only 150 yards, he saw the bear and shot it through the ear. He said Rainy heard the shot and came back to help him load it into the truck.

"We found a gut pile in the woods," I said. "Your bear?"

"Yup. I gutted it out in the basement and dumped the entrails in the woods."

"Why not gut it out where you killed it?" I asked.

Brian stuffed his hands in his pockets and shrugged absently.

"So, it was just you and Rainy who loaded the bear into the truck, right?

"Yup."

I had to suppress a smile knowing it would be an impossible task for two men of their limited physical abilities. I asked Brian if he would take me to the location where he shot the bear so we could verify that it wasn't killed near their baited cabin. Brian said he wouldn't be able to find the place but that he thought Rainy could. According to Brian, Rainy knew the area quite well, and had suggested that he hunt the very location where the bear was killed. However, when I asked Rainy, he refused to cooperate in any way.

By now, Darrel and Bob had finished photographing the entrails, including a close-up of the corn-filled stomach, so we walked back to the feeder to look for blood on the ground but found nothing. We were about to leave when Bill noticed faint tire impressions in the grass going from the feeder toward the cabin located some forty yards away. After following for a short distance, we discovered a tiny pool of blood hidden deep within the grassy turf between the tire tracks. As we continued following the trail, more traces of blood were discovered.

When the trail ended at the basement door, I was certain the bear had been shot at the feeder, then loaded into Rainy's pickup truck and transported there.

With that in mind, we went back to the feeder and scraped back the ground surface, uncovering gobs of blood-soaked corn kernels that had been covered up by raking leaves and dirt over the area.

We had some good evidence, but it wasn't enough. Brian and Rainy could claim that they placed the bear carcass near the feeder for photographs, or whatever. Also, many camps in the area have active corn feeders, a plausible explanation for corn in the animal's stomach. We needed more, and I just didn't see where we were going to get it.

It was then that deputy Bob McConnell called me over to the corn feeder. He was lying on the ground, examining a support beam with two bullet holes spaced about one inch apart. Bullets, or fragments thereof, were imbedded inside the holes and black hairs were poking out.

We carefully extracted them from the wooden beam. The first cavity contained a mutilated high-caliber copper jacket. The second held a lead bullet core that had completely separated from its jacket. A short black hair protruded from a fold in the disfigured lead. What's more, there were traces of blood only inches away! I now had all of the pieces of the puzzle that I needed. I was certain the Pennsylvania State

Police Crime Lab would be able to verify that the hair and blood were from a bear. However, what I didn't count on was a cunning defense attorney who would later claim that I fabricated the evidence.

Brian and Rainy were watching us from the cabin, but they had no idea we found the bullet (in two pieces) that killed their trophy bear. They didn't know the bullet had passed through the bear's head, because it exited   through its ear without leaving a mark. I motioned for them to come over and said that I believed their bear was killed unlawfully through the use of bait. I then explained that charges would be filed as soon as the crime lab completed analyzing the evidence we collected. The men refused to admit any wrongdoing, so we seized the bear as evidence (over their objections) and departed. Although there were two bags of ice in the animal's chest cavity, the carcass was already spoiled due to the unusually mild temperatures over the previous 36 hours.

After transporting the bear to the Game Commission's Northcentral Regional Office and placing it in a large walk-in freezer, I forwarded everything we collected to the State Police Crime Lab in Harrisburg. I needed a ballistics test done to determine the caliber of the bullet we recovered from the feeder. I also wanted the hair and blood we found scientifically documented as belonging to a black bear.

A month went by before I received a report from the crime lab. Corporal Wayne Poust, a ballistics expert, was able to determine that the copper jacket came from a .30 caliber class ball. However, it was impossible to verify the exact caliber due to the extent of mutilation that occurred. I knew that Brain Brainfreez used a .308 caliber rifle to kill the bear, so at least we were in the ball park.

Paul Daubey, a criminologist working in the crime lab's chemistry section, was able to determine that the blood and hair came from a black bear. He was also able to confirm that the hairs had specifically come from the head and ear area of a bear. After reviewing the crime lab report, I charged Brian with killing a bear through the use of bait and the unlawful transportation of a bear illegally killed. Rainy was also charged with unlawful transportation of the bear.

The defendants hired an attorney and a trial was scheduled. I had twenty exhibits to introduce as evidence, and expected at least ten witnesses would testify between the prosecution and defense. I usually prosecuted cases myself at the district judge level, but felt it would be unwise in this instance, so I asked the district attorney to assign someone from his office. The defense had hired a sharp attorney, and I knew I'd be subjected to intense cross-examination as the arresting officer. Under the circumstances, acting as both the prosecutor and witness would not be in the best interest of the Commonwealth.

Frederick Lingle, a former district attorney, was selected to represent the Commonwealth on my behalf. Fred was, and still is, a sincere and accomplished attorney with many years of experience in criminal law. His knowledge and craftiness would be needed against the sly, manipulative attorney hired by the defendants.

The trial was scheduled for early February in Renovo, some three months after the violations occurred. A few days prior, Ranger and I discussed the evidence we were going to present. Ranger had a bachelor's degree in biology, and had previously been declared an expert witness by the court in matters concerning deer biology. He suggested we examine the bear carcass for corn in the esophagus. If any was found, it would strengthen our case. I called the regional office and had the bear removed from the freezer to allow for some thawing, and we stopped by to inspect the mouth and esophagus the next day. The bear was still mostly frozen, making the examination difficult, but we were able to find a few tiny pieces of masticated corn in its teeth and esophagus.

The trial came off as scheduled and lasted nearly four hours. Our evidence was overwhelming. However, the defendants managed to get a couple of their friends to come to the trial and lie for them. They swore under oath they saw Brian and Rainy with a bear in Rainy's truck three miles from Camp

Chug-a-Lug on the day it was shot. In addition, Brian claimed that the blood we found at the feeder came from Rainy's pickup truck when he swept it out after transporting the bear. Brian also testified that there was no exit wound from the bear's head, so the bullet we found couldn't be from his bear. Our position was that the bullet passed through the opposite ear, so there would be no clearly visible exit wound. When all was said and done, District Judge McDermott found both of the defendants guilty. Their attorney immediately filed for an appeal.

A month later, their attorney represented some other defendants in a different Game Law case. This case involved the killing of a deer within 30 feet of a baited area in Game Warden John Hancock's district. As in my case, the defendants claimed their deer was shot and wounded a considerable distance from the bait, claiming it ran hundreds of yards after it was shot only to drop dead 30 feet from the corn pile.

Warden Hancock asked Ranger to examine the deer and testify in the case for him. Ranger agreed, and after inspecting the carcass, found that the deer's spinal cord had been severed by a bullet. It was his expert opinion that it was impossible for the deer to move from where it was initially shot. The defense attorney lost the case and filed an appeal. Soon afterwards he filed a "discovery" petition before the Court directing the Game Commission to produce both the deer and the Camp Chug-a-Lug bear for examination by a local veterinarian. The purpose for the petition was for an opposing opinion as to the accuracy of Ranger's previous testimony in each case.

Normally, we would have complied without an argument, but the deer carcass had been given to a needy family. All that remained was the head and hide, and Special Prosecutor Fred Lingle had to show cause why the petition should not be granted or the deer case would certainly be lost. Fred argued that the "discovery rule" did not apply to either the deer case, or the Camp Chug-a-lug bear case.

Judge Carson V. Brown issued a seven-page opinion and order agreeing with the Commonwealths argument. We were not required to relinquish the deer or the bear carcass to the defendants. However, I believed the defendants in my case were going to argue in their upcoming court appeal that there was no exit wound in the bear's head, making it impossible for us to have recovered a bullet that penetrated the skull.

I decided to have the head X-rayed by Dr. Lester Beck, a veterinarian in Williamsport. Dr. Beck's examination showed a scattering of tiny bullet fragments traveling in a direct path from ear to ear. The fragments were so small, and so few in number, that it was clearly evident most of the bullet had exited the skull. Unfortunately, Dr. Beck had a policy of not testifying in such matters, and made that known to us before consenting to do the examination. He did give us the X-ray and a written report, but we thought it was unlikely the documents would be allowed by the court without the doctor's actual testimony.

The Common Pleas Court trial began as scheduled in May, and we were confident there was enough circumstantial evidence to prove the bear was unlawfully killed. There were many exhibits to be introduced. Testimony in the trial continued through the entire day, and resumed the following morning. Undoubtedly, our best evidence was the bear hairs embedded in the wooden feeder and in the folds of the mangled bullet. State Police Criminologist Paul Daubey testified that the hair in the lead bullet core came specifically from the ear of a bear. He based this upon an analysis of the narrowness of the hair, its modulation, color, and scaling. In addition, we testified that corn was found in the mouth and esophagus of the bear carcass.

The defense presented a Veterinarian as an expert witness on their behalf. This self-proclaimed authority on bears testified that it was a common occurrence for a bear to regurgitate when it was killed. Thus, their explanation for the corn we found in the mouth and esophagus of the bear. The veterinarian based this opinion on his personal examination of only five dead bears during his career.

Ranger and I later refuted this by explaining we never observed a dead bear that regurgitated, and that between the two of us, we had examined hundreds of bears' mouths while removing a premolar tooth to determine their age.

The defense also argued that there were over a hundred bullet holes in the feeder because it was often used as a target practice backstop. They also reminded the court that according to our testimony, bears were visiting the feeder on a daily basis. They claimed the hairs in the wood fibers were from bears brushing against the splintered wood. They also argued that the hair protruding from the lead bullet core resulted from the bullet striking the hair-laden support beam during target practice.

We shattered their target practice theory when we testified that the lead core had separated from the metal jacket *before* entering the support beam. A lead bullet core can only separate from its metal jacket while penetrating an object, in this case, the bear's head. The metal jacket peeled off as the bullet passed through the skull, resulting in two separate fragments striking the feeder.

After two days of testimony, the special prosecutor and defense attorney were ready to give their closing arguments. However, the judge instructed the attorneys to file written summaries on the case instead. He also instructed that they would each be permitted to file a rebuttal brief against the opposing attorney's closing summary.

The defense attorney filed an eleven page summary in support of a finding of innocence while the special prosecutor filed an eleven page summary in support of a finding of guilt. Following this, the defense filed a seven page rebuttal brief, and the special prosecutor submitted an eight page rebuttal brief.

The written position of the defense was as follows:

- Wasserman considered the defendants to be guilty until they proved themselves innocent.

- Wasserman denied the defendants the opportunity to present evidence in their defense (the bear carcass).

- The Commonwealth's evidence was purely circumstantial.

- The Commonwealth's 20 exhibits of evidence proved nothing.

- The corn in the bear's mouth and esophagus was regurgitated corn.

- The blood at the feeder had been caused by sweeping out the pickup truck that transported the bear.

- The bear hairs found in the bullet holes in the feeder were caused by bears brushing against splintered wood.

- Two witnesses observed the defendants in possession of the bear three miles from the defendant's camp.

- Bullets found in the feeder were from target practice.

- The court should not rule out the possibility that the recovered bullets were manufactured by the Commonwealth.

- Wasserman did whatever was necessary to find evidence that his belief of an illegal kill was right.

- Wasserman would say or do anything to get a conviction in this case.

- The overzealous prosecution of this case casts doubt on the credibility of the Commonwealth's evidence.

- The Commonwealth manipulated the evidence.

- Wasserman had a conviction-at-any-price approach in the case.

- Wasserman demonstrated extreme bias and prejudice towards these defendants, which the defense believes has colored his testimony.

- The Commonwealth's refusal to allow the scientific testing of the bear carcass must be taken as proof that the Commonwealth's testimony regarding the bear is false.

The written position of the prosecution was as follows:

- Brian Brainfreez shot a bear on the opening day of the season well before opening hour (Sunday night-Monday morning).

- The bear had corn in its throat, esophagus and stomach, indicating that it was eating corn when it was killed.

- The corn feeder at Camp Chug-a-lug had a fresh lead bullet core and steel jacket of the .30 caliber class embedded in a wooden support beam.

- Brian Brainfreez used a .30 caliber class rifle (.308) to shoot the bear.

- Hairs from the head and ear area of a bear were embedded inside the bullet holes created by the lead core and steel jacket.

- A hair from the ear of a bear was embedded within the mutilated lead bullet core.

- The bear in question had been shot through the ears.

- The recovered bullet had been fired from the direction of the defendant's cabin.

- There was bear blood on the feeder and soaked into the ground at the feeder.

- The surface of the ground immediately in front of the feeder had no blood on it, indicating it had been covered or raked in order to conceal evidence of an illegal kill.

- There was a trail of bear blood and tire impressions from the feeder to the camp basement entrance.

- Another trail of blood went from the basement door to a spot in the woods some 100 yards away, ending at the entrails of the bear.

- The entrails were concealed to cover-up a crime.

- Brian and Rainy defied logic by refusing to show the game wardens the location they claimed to have killed and dragged out the bear.

- The two witnesses that testified they saw the bear in the defendant's possession some 3 miles from Camp Chug-a-lug lied.

- The two defendants could not drag a 400 pound bear to their truck and load it by themselves as they claimed.

- The defense attorney had a vivid imagination, which caused him to attack the prosecuting officer's credibility and integrity.

Several months later, Judge Carson V. Brown issued a 16-page opinion and order on the case. The judge stated that the Commonwealth's evidence was circumstantial. However, in sifting through and evaluating the evidence as a whole, the court concluded the guilt of both defendants was established beyond a reasonable doubt. The judge said the defense made the mistake of taking each piece of circumstantial evidence separately, and attempting to argue that each isolated item of evidence by itself did not establish guilt beyond a reasonable doubt. However, the court was obligated to consider all of the circumstantial evidence as a whole, and determined the Commonwealth met its burden of guilt beyond a reasonable doubt.

Brian and Rainy each received heavy fines and had their hunting privileges revoked for three years. In addition, they spent thousands in attorney fees—an un*bear*able price to pay for an attorney who said so much, while accomplishing so little.

We reached the old wolf in time to watch a fierce green fire dying in her eyes. I realized then, and have known ever since, that there was something new to me in those eyes – something known only to her and to the mountain. I was young then and full of trigger itch. I thought that because fewer wolves meant more deer, then no wolves would mean hunters' paradise. But after seeing the fire die, I sensed that neither the wolf nor the mountain agreed with such a view.
~Aldo Leopold

BIG NASTY

A PICKUP TRUCK WAS STOPPED on the road just ahead with the passenger door wide open. I could see a hunter in the field to my left, a place I had released pheasants the day before. The pheasant season opened tomorrow morning, and my first thought was that the hunter might be getting a head start. I pulled up behind the truck, and Ranger and I got out of my patrol car. The hunter spotted us, then turned and walked in our direction. As he approached, I shouted for him to unload his shotgun and he immediately complied. As he bent over to pick up the ejected rounds, the driver's door of the pickup swung open. Out stepped a very big man, his face flushed with rage.

Both men walked within several feet of us and stopped. I asked the man with the shotgun what he was hunting for, and he said grouse. The big man just stood there, rock solid, his facial expression slowly relaxing. He had the tattoo of a rattlesnake coiled around his neck, the head on one side, tail on the other. The mouth was wide open with huge, pointy fangs, its tail raised up with 16 rattles. He wore his hair in a tight Mohawk, four inches wide and one inch high, his head shaved clean to the scalp on each side. The man's cheekbones were pronounced and high, his eyes dark and intense. A razor-like scar flowed across the bridge of his nose and down the left side of his face. His forearms were thick and vascular, almost the same size as his huge upper arms. Frank Frazetta's epic painting of Conan the Barbarian came to mind.

"It's unusual to find a grouse in a field," I said to the hunter. "They're a woodland bird." I was convinced he was after pheasants, but I had no proof.

"So what. You gonna arrest me?" he snapped back.

"I just want to have a look at your hunting license," I said.

"Oh, yes sir Mr. Game Warden," he said as he turned around. I removed the license from the holder pinned to his jacket and examined it. He was a local man named Peter Piker.

"Okay, you're good," I said, stuffing the license back in place. "But I want to advise you that I stocked pheasants in that field for the opening day tomorrow, so I suggest you hunt in the adjacent woodland for grouse."

"Yeah, whatever you say Mr. Game Warden," he said bitterly. "Tell you what, maybe someday I'll see you when you're off duty, and maybe you'll wish we hadn't met."

"Is that a threat?"

"It's a promise."

"Tell you what," I said. "Since being stupid isn't a crime, I'm going to let you go home to mommy now."

Piker's jaw dropped. He said nothing, just stood there blinking foolishly. The big man looked at me and smiled. "Let's go," he said, smacking Piker on the back of his head. Ranger and I stood there and watched as they walked back to the truck and drove away.

"Do you know who the big guy was?" Ranger asked with some concern.

"No idea."

"That was Big Nasty."

"Never heard of him," I said. "So, you know the guy?"

"No, but I've heard a lot about him, and I watched him in action once." Ranger said. "I was having a beer in a taproom near Williamsport. Three bikers and their girlfriends were sitting on stools at the bar. They were wearing colors (gang affiliation patches). Big Nasty had been drinking hard, when suddenly he climbs up on the bar and stands there grinning down at the bikers. He rips off his shirt, and he's covered with tattoos; one is a big bear trap completely covering his chest. The bikers think it's funny at first, but then he starts kicking their beer mugs off the bar, one by one."

"That's nuts! What did they do to him?" I asked.

"Nothing. They walked out."

"So, Big Nasty is a gang leader?"

"No. He was born and raised here, has ten brothers, they grew up poor. Lived off the land in a log cabin. That was before you were assigned here. Most of his brothers have moved to other parts of the state. They grew up hungry and ate a lot of venison. I remember watching Big Nasty along Young Woman's Creek one day eating live crawfish when he was a teenager."

"Wow, a rough life," I said.

"Yeah, it was. Their idea of fun was competing to see who could do the most pullups from a tree branch or a foot race to the top of the mountain. He's a natural athlete, six-foot-five and 275 pounds. And he's mean. I can't believe he smiled when you came back at his friend. That just ain't like him at all."

"Well thanks for the warning. I guess I'll be careful if we meet again, but I just didn't get a bad feeling from the guy."

The following year, I ran into Big Nasty again. I was getting a lot of road hunting complaints from folks who lived and hunted in the Kettle Creek area. Some hunters were cruising the roads looking for deer and shooting from their vehicles, so I decided to set up a decoy operation. Using a mounted deer from a taxidermy shop, I set it in the area where most of the complaints were coming from. It was a standing doe that I placed in some brush behind a small Hawthorne tree. I didn't want it to stand out and entice someone who wasn't already predisposed to hunting from a motor vehicle. You had to be road hunting, looking hard to see this decoy.

Ranger was dressed in camouflage and hidden near the roadway close to the decoy. I was in my patrol car, concealed and ready to pursue anyone who tried to escape from Ranger. Within the first few hours, we apprehended two men that shot at the decoy from inside their vehicles. In each case, Ranger would step out of the bushes and loudly identify himself immediately after a shot was fired. He would then approach the vehicle and secure any firearms found inside before escorting the violator to my position where I would write a citation or arrange for a settlement by field acknowledgment of guilt.

We were about to call it off when Ranger announced on his portable radio that another vehicle was approaching. I held tight, rolled down my windows and listened. I could hear the vehicle creeping along very slowly, when suddenly it stopped.

"Got a white Ford pickup," called Ranger. "Two men. They drove past the decoy and stopped." He paused for a long moment before speaking again. "Now somebody is getting out of the passenger side. He has a rifle. I can't believe it! He's crawling up the road on his belly for a better shot at the decoy."

BOOM!

The echo from a high-powered rifle rebounded from hillside to hillside through the broad valley. Moments later, Ranger was transmitting again on his portable radio.

"I'm bringing them over to you now. It's Big Nasty and one of his brothers. Big Nasty shot at the decoy. So far they're complying, but his brother is almost as big as he is. This could get ugly."

"Ten-four. After you bring them to me, I want you to go back and position yourself at the decoy."

"What! Did you hear what I said?"

"Yes I did. Just secure their firearms and tell Big Nasty to get in my patrol car. I'll take it from there."

"Okay, boss. I hope you know what you're doing."

Ranger pulled up to my location and parked with the Ford pickup truck immediately behind him. As Big Nasty got out of the truck, I pushed open my passenger door and motioned for him to get in. He walked over and squeezed inside my car, sitting with his knees pressed against the dashboard, his head almost touching the roof. "Seat go back?" he grunted as he groped for a release lever.

"It's back as far as it'll go." I said.

I glanced out the windshield and waved Ranger away but he shook his head and stayed put.

Big Nasty sat in silence and looked straight ahead as if deep in thought. I was a bit intimidated by his enormous size, but I wouldn't dare show it. I was a big man too, a 220-pound powerlifter, but this guy was a genetic freak of nature. Then, before I could say anything, Big Nasty began to laugh while still looking straight ahead.

"I can't believe I thought it was a real deer!" he said with a broad grin. "Can I look and see where I hit it?" Although his demeanor was calm, he was almost shouting as he spoke, but I sensed that this was normal for him.

"No use," I replied. "That decoy looks like Swiss cheese with all the bullet holes from other hunters."

Big turned his head and looked at me. "I'm glad I'm not the only one that got fooled," he said with a chuckle. "I shouldn't have shot at it, but it's the last day and I really wanted to take a deer home. I'll pay the fine. No argument; you got me cold."

"Well, at least you got out of the truck and tried to sneak up on it," I said. "Everyone else just rolled down their window and shot from the vehicle. That would have been a much larger penalty. Still, the law says you have to be twenty-five yards from the road after leaving a vehicle before you can shoot."

"I know I was wrong." Big Nasty replied. "I just wanted to bring a deer home to my wife and little girl. She's six years old. My little sweetheart."

"I appreciate where you're coming from, but I treat everyone the same with decoy deer violations, and it's a hundred dollar fine."

"I understand," he said, shaking his head with regret.

"Six years old?"

"Huh?"

"Your daughter," I said. "I have two small children at home myself."

He nodded thoughtfully.

"Look," I said, "It's only a week until Christmas, so spend the money on your little girl for now and we can square up some time next month. Normally it's ten days for settlement, but I'll think of something to explain the delay to my supervisor."

"Sir, you have no idea how much I appreciate that," he said. "If there's anything I can do for you, just say the word."

I was surprised by Big's attitude; he wasn't anything like his reputation. "I'll keep that in mind," I said. "I didn't expect this from you. I was warned about your temper. That you can be hostile."

Big looked away for a few seconds, and then snapped his head back toward me with a fierce glare in his eyes. At that moment, I was glad Ranger was standing nearby. Before I could speak again, he replied, and the fire in his eyes dimmed.

"I have a lot of respect for you because of the way you handled Pete Piker," he said. "He's a fighter, and he can be a real jerk, but you stood up to him. So I'll be straight with you. I'm an alcoholic and I've done things that I regret."

"Sorry," I interrupted. "I shouldn't have mentioned it."

"In a way, I'm glad you did," Big Nasty replied with a sigh. "A few years ago, I moved away from here to work construction. It's a long story, but after getting fired, then finding another job and getting fired again, I quit drinking. When I was drinking, I was nasty. I did things that I'm not proud of. But those days are over. I'll always be considered an alcoholic, but I'll never go back to drinking alcohol. It's an addiction, and I'm proud that I beat it. My family is what's important to me now."

I nodded that I understood.

"I moved back here last year with my wife and daughter," he continued. "I love it here. I was born and raised here. But I have a bad reputation because of my past."

"Do you have a job?"

"Yep, working construction with my brother. Things are slow right now, but we're getting by." Big reached into his shirt pocket and pulled out a photograph. "Here's a picture of my little girl."

"She's cute," I said. My daughter Erika was the same age, so they would have been in school together, no doubt sharing some of the same classes at Renovo Elementary School. It was a small school with less than 200 children in kindergarten through sixth grade. I was glad Big felt that he could talk to me about his personal life, and I wished we could have met under better circumstances. There was no doubt in my mind he was serious when he offered help if I needed it.

"Big, I have a spike buck hanging at my home," I said. "It's skinned and dressed out. It was turned in by a hunter who shot it in mistake for a doe. I'll drop it off at your home tomorrow morning." Big looked stunned as he offered a hand the size of a catcher's mitt and we shook.

"Thanks John, you have no idea what this means to me and my family," he said. "I'll see you tomorrow." Big opened the door and began to step out of my car, then paused and turned toward me

"Can I ask you a question?"

"Sure."

"Where'd that bullet in your ashtray come from? It looks like a .22 caliber that was dug out of something, like a carcass."

"It came from one of three deer that were shot and dumped behind Joey's bar a year ago. All three were shot in the head. They weren't dressed out and none of the meat was taken."

"Do you know who did it?"

"We have our suspicions but nothing solid."

"That really makes me mad when someone shoots a deer and leaves it lay. But three of them! That's awful!"

Big thanked me again, climbed out of my vehicle and walked over to his brother's truck. He smiled and nodded at Ranger just before getting inside. Ranger turned his head in my direction, his eyebrows raised as if to say, *what the heck just happened?* He hurried over to the passenger side of my patrol car, opened the door and leaned inside.

"What the heck just happened?"

"I knew you were going to say that," I replied with a chuckle. "It's getting late, let's pack up and I'll explain everything while we take the decoy down."

The following week, I got a phone call from Joey, the Renovo bartender where the three illegal deer had been dumped. He told me that Big Nasty just left his bar after a long talk. Joey said that Big was one of his best customers many years ago.

"I saw him!" Joey blurted.

"Saw who?"

"Coyotee Boy! I watched him dump the deer carcasses behind my bar that night, and I'll testify in court if you need me to."

I was shocked when he told me this. The last time I talked to him, he said he suspected Coyotee Boy had killed the deer but didn't see anything. He also made it clear that he was afraid of Coyotee Boy.

"What made you decide to come forward with this?"

"Two bad choices," he said. "Did I want Coyotee Boy mad at me, or Big Nasty? The decision was easy."

I thanked Joey and told him I would keep his name off the search warrant for Coyotee Boy's rifle. However, I would need to reveal it to the Judge.

The following morning, Ranger and I secured a search warrant and went to Coyotee Boy's home in Renovo. Ranger covered the back while I went to the front door and rapped on it with my fist.

"What do you want?" Coyotee Boy shouted from behind the door.

"State game warden. Open up, I have a search warrant!"

"What if I don't?"

"I'll break your door down with a wood-splitting maul."

I heard a deadbolt slide back from inside and stepped away as the door swung open. Coyotee Boy wasn't a boy; he was in his mid-thirties, although he looked much younger than his years. He was thin, about 5'10" with greasy brown hair that fell to his shoulders. His face was round and covered in freckles, his eyes dark and brooding. I handed him the warrant as Ranger walked around to my position and we stepped inside.

Coyotee Boy's wife stood a few feet behind him. She was thin, frail and visibly trembling.

"No need to worry ma'am," I said. "We're just here for his .22 caliber firearms, and then we will leave."

She pointed to a wooden gun cabinet in the corner of the room. "He keeps everything in there."

Coyotee Boy looked at the warrant and saw it concerned the three deer he dumped behind Joey's bar.

"Who's the confidential informant listed on the warrant?" he demanded.

"I can't tell you that," I said. "But he will testify in court if necessary."

"Somebody's gonna regret this," he said angrily.

"It's gonna be you regretting this." I said. "Any threat or act of violence against a potential witness is a felony, and you will end up in jail."

"You don't scare me!" he said with a sneer of contempt. "I've been in jail before! It's my home away from home."

Ranger and I ignored his comment and began our search. We found two .22 caliber rifles, one in the gun cabinet and another in their bedroom. I handed Coyotee Boy a receipt for the guns and we walked out the door.

Two months later, I received a report from the Pennsylvania State Police Ballistics Lab. We had a confirmation that one of the rifles we submitted had fired the bullet we removed from one of the carcasses. Now the evidence was overwhelming. We had an eyewitness and a crime lab report that would corroborate his testimony. I filed citations for unlawfully killing three deer, and Coyotee Boy pleaded not guilty. A trial was scheduled for two weeks later.

On the day of the trial, I entered the courtroom with Pennsylvania State Trooper Smith from the Crime Lab. Coyotee Boy was seated at the defendant's table on the left side of the courtroom. I was surprised that he didn't have an attorney. Then I realized he was probably there for one purpose: to find out who was going to testify against him. He had a reputation for being a psycho, and I was worried for Joey's safety even though I had warned Coyotee Boy to stay away from him.

The trial was supposed to begin at 11:00 AM. It was ten after eleven, and Joey hadn't appeared yet. In five more minutes, the trial would begin with or without him. I didn't know if the judge would honor my request to reschedule the hearing if he didn't show up, and I was beginning to worry.

At 11:15 AM Joey walked into the courtroom and sat down beside me. He was very nervous. Coyotee Boy was staring at him like a junkyard dog protecting his turf. The judge hadn't walked in yet, and I told Coyotee Boy to back off. He ignored me and continued to stare at Joey. Joey began breathing heavily, and I could see a line of sweat running down the side of his face. He was visibly shaken, and wouldn't look at Coyotee Boy. When Joey whispered to me that he was starting to feel sick, I knew what that meant. He was getting cold feet and my case was about to fall apart.

Then came Big Nasty. He lowered his head as he stepped through the doorway and walked directly to Joey. Joey stood up. Now he was at ease. Big Nasty embraced him with his right arm and slapped his back twice with his left hand. Big smiled at me briefly, and then frowned. His facial expression changed from tranquility to rage. I saw the fire in his eyes as he turned and faced Coyotee Boy.

Coyote Boy quickly turned his head and looked down at the desk in front of him. He tried to hide it, but I could see a slight shiver in his shoulders. Joey had nothing to fear from Coyotee Boy. Big Nasty, without saying a word, sent an unmistakable message.

The judge entered the courtroom and we all stood until given the order to be seated. The judge read the charges aloud and asked Coyotee Boy how he would plead.

"Guilty, Your Honor. I did it, and I would like to request time payments."

The judge was surprised. He expected a trial. But there would be no need on this day, as the evidence and the citizen support was overwhelming. Coyotee Boy paid a heavy fine, and his hunting and trapping privileges were revoked for several years.

And that should be where my story ends with Coyotee Boy. But it was just the beginning, as I had many encounters with him in later years.

A few weeks later, I was stopped along Route 120 near Hyner for a road killed bear, but it was easily over 500 pounds and too big for me to handle alone. I was about to call for assistance when a Ford pickup truck pulled to the shoulder of the road just behind me. It was Big Nasty. "Hey John," he called, "need some help?"

"Sure do!" I replied. "Its legs are so thick I can't wrap my hands around them."

Big Nasty climbed out of the truck, walked over and helped me lift the bear onto the big game rack on the back of my vehicle. Afterwards, we stood there and talked for a long time. We were surprised to learn that we had a lot in common. Although we were both family men, we were also loners, preferring to avoid the company of others. But in a strange way, two men who should have been at odds with each other, seemed to be forming a bond.

Several months later, on a hot summer afternoon, I was contacted by a Pennsylvania Fish & Boat Commission Warden. He had a search warrant for Big Nasty's home, and asked me to assist him. Big lived in a trailer back in the woods along Young Woman's Creek and had a rattlesnake for a pet, which was against the law. The fish warden and a deputy met me near the entrance to Big Nasty's dirt-covered driveway and we spoke briefly. I volunteered to serve the warrant, so we drove down the long driveway and parked in front of his trailer. As we approached the front door, the fish wardens were whispering to each other, so I turned and asked if anything was wrong.

"What caused all the dents in the aluminum siding on the trailer?"

"Big gets upset sometimes and throws some punches." I said. "No worries, he's not doing that anymore."

"Well how about that beat-up Chevy back by the woods? Why is the roof caved in?"

"That's old too." I answered. "Big broke some bones in his hand, so he doesn't punch automobiles anymore."

I knocked on the door, and moments later Big's wife opened it. "He thinks you're going to take him to jail," she said. "He's in the bedroom; he won't come out."

"Hey Big!" I hollered. "We aren't going to arrest you, we just want the rattlesnake. You have my word." I was watching the hallway in the trailer, and soon Big walked out of the bedroom.

"Okay, I know it's illegal," he said. "Come on I'll show you where it is."

We followed him to the living room, and he pointed to the snake. It was in a brightly lit aquarium directly under a cage that held a very lively gray squirrel. The fish wardens took possession of the snake and handed him a citation. I told Big that I'd be back the next day for the gray squirrel, as it was illegal to possess that too.

The following morning I went to Big Nasty's home for the squirrel. Big was expecting me, and he opened the door before I could knock. I walked inside and saw his young daughter sitting on the floor near the squirrel cage.

"Daddy rescued the squirrel," she cried. "It was hurt along the road and he saved it."

"Okay honey," I said. "Don't cry. I'm not going to take it." I looked at Big and said, "Listen, legally I gotta tell you to release it."

Big frowned and shrugged his shoulders. "I understand you're just doing your job, John. How much is the fine gonna cost me?"

"There isn't going to be a fine." I said. "I believe what your little girl told me. But you can't keep it inside. If you release it, it'll still hang around your house because you've been feeding it for a while."

Big Nasty nodded that he understood.

"By the way, I'm not coming back, if you know what I mean."

Big's little girl jumped up and gave me a hug. Then Big Nasty hugged me, too! It was the first and only time that a man outside my family ever did that.

And we became friends for life that day. The best of friends.

The last word in ignorance is the man who says of an animal or plant: 'What good is it?'
~Aldo Leopold

COYOTEE BOY

The weekend prior to deer season has introduced many unusual experiences during my career as a state game warden. Sometimes when people travel into this remote area from other more populated regions, they become overwhelmed by the solitude and seclusion that can be found here. Most of them enjoy the experience and have great respect for the land and the people who live here. Unfortunately, there is an attitude that prevails with some folks, that the backwoods are inhabited by a bunch of uneducated hillbillies who are unsophisticated in their ways.

It was on a Saturday just before buck season back in 1988 that Ranger and I found it necessary to provide an attitude adjustment. We were on night patrol well after the legal hour for spotlighting, and had just passed a local bar, when an old four-wheel-drive International Scout pulled behind us. The Scout caught up quickly and began tailgating my rear bumper. I was annoyed, but since we were about to make a turn onto a steep mountain road, I tried to ignore the glare of its headlights.

The road was just ahead, and as I turned off the main highway the old Scout followed closely behind. I pulled over to allow it to pass, and when the Scout went by I observed three occupants seated inside. As soon as I pulled out behind it, a man in the back seat held a spotlight out the window and started spotlighting the forest to my left. Before I had a chance to react, he swung the spotlight backward and cast the

153

powerful beam directly into my face, temporarily blinding me. I couldn't believe it! We were in a marked patrol car with a red emergency light on the roof and in full uniform.

The Scout sped away and I quickly gave chase, but as Ranger reached under the dash to turn on the emergency light, the switch fell apart in his hand! The Scout's spotlight continued to shine into my windshield, its unrelenting glare forcing me to keep my distance as I continued my pursuit up the winding mountain road. Ranger was frantically trying to put the switch back together as I chased the suspects, all the while wondering why they would commit such a flagrant violation of the Game Law after passing us. It was as though they were taunting us, luring me to pull them over.

I recalled a similar incident that occurred just two years before in Apollo, Pennsylvania. Two individuals in a car began circling around a police cruiser that had been parked along an isolated township road. The subjects began shouting obscenities at the police officer as they squealed their tires and drove about in a reckless manner. The officer gave chase and pulled them over, but when he approached their car, he was shot and killed. The driver had a demented craving to kill a cop, and the 21-year-old rookie officer fell right into his trap.

"I got it!" Ranger shouted as blazing red beams of light reflected off the trees embracing the narrow road ahead. The man in the back seat quickly turned off his spotlight but the driver had no intention of stopping. However, the old Scout was no match for my patrol car, and I quickly squeezed beside it on a straight stretch of roadway near the top of the mountain. Ranger leaned out the window and barked the command to pull over, but the driver ignored him. The road began getting very steep, and the Scout seemed to be losing momentum. I knew that this was my best opportunity to overtake them, and managed to get my car in front of the Scout, forcing it to a stop. Our main concern at that moment was the disadvantage of being clearly illuminated by the Scout's headlights. We had to take control, and we had to do it quickly and decisively. Because of their bizarre behavior, I considered them to be a potential threat to our personal safety.

Ranger and I exited my patrol car and approached opposite sides of the Scout. Ranger ordered the occupant on the passenger side to get out and put his hands on the roof, and the subject immediately complied. Unfortunately, I wasn't having the same success with the driver. I ordered him out of the vehicle, but he ignored me. I opened the door and again gave him the command to get out, but he just sat there staring at me. His left hand was on the steering wheel while his right was out of view. This concerned me, as did the intentions of the man in the back seat with the spotlight. Because it was dark inside the Scout, I could only see his silhouette.

"Let's go!" I shouted as I reached in and grabbed the driver. He refused to budge so I yanked him out of the car. He reeked of booze, and was obviously intoxicated, which caused him to fall face down onto the paved roadway before I could catch him. After giving him a quick pat down to make sure he was unarmed, I turned around for the man in the back seat. But before I took my first step, the old Scout popped out of gear and began coasting down the steep mountain road in reverse! Ranger and his suspect were knocked to the ground by the open passenger door as I sprinted after the runaway vehicle and tried to get inside, but it was moving too quickly.

"Dive for the brake!" I shouted at the man in the back as I ran alongside the Scout and grabbed the door handle. I was hoping he would lunge between the bucket seats in the front and hit the brake pedal, but he froze. I refused to let go of the door handle and was being dragged along the road while I continued to shout at the man to dive for the brake. I could feel extreme heat on my feet as my leather boots were grinding away from the hard-surfaced roadway. There was no guardrail on this dangerous stretch of roadway, and if the car went over the edge it would plunge down the mountainside causing serious bodily injury or death to the occupant. Although his reckless attempt to blind me with the spotlight was unforgivable, I took no pleasure from the predicament he was in. I felt helpless as the Scout veered toward the edge of the mountain. Realizing there was nothing I could do except save myself, I let go of the door and rolled, the front tires barely missing my legs as the Scout slipped by me.

I heard the Scout hit something hard as I picked myself up off the ground. Fortunately, a large oak tree prevented the car from dropping over the steep side-hill. Up until that moment, I never dreamed that a car smashing into a tree could create such a feeling of relief.

Hoping the passenger wasn't injured, I ran over to the Scout and shined my flashlight inside. I couldn't believe my eyes when I saw Coyotee Boy sitting in the back seat, still holding the spotlight. Although he was badly shaken from the ordeal, he suffered no serious injuries.

Ranger and I gathered them all together and it was obvious they had been drinking heavily, so I contacted the state police and had them send a patrol car. After questioning the driver, they transported him to the hospital for a blood alcohol test and found that the alcohol in his bloodstream was well above the legal limit. The defendants eventually pleaded guilty to a variety of Game Law violations, and during a subsequent trial, the driver was found guilty of driving under the influence of alcohol. It is a rare individual indeed who can cause both his hunting license and driver's license to be revoked from one single incident.

Coyotee Boy was still under suspension of his hunting and trapping privileges from the three deer he killed and dumped at Joey's bar, and this incident added two more years.

The following hunting season, I discovered he was hunting in neighboring Potter County with his brother Wolfe. Wolfe was a poacher too, but not nearly as bad as Coyotee Boy. Wolfe was friendly, always waved to me, and if I saw him in town he would usually strike up a conversation. He knew I wouldn't cut him any slack if I caught him; Wolfe looked at life as though we were competing against each other in a sport. And while he wanted to win the game, there'd be no grudge if he lost.

Wolfe and Coyotee Boy would road-hunt the big woods of Potter County with only one rifle in the car, and that rifle belonged to Wolfe. It was the perfect cover for Coyotee Boy, who could easily state that he wasn't hunting if the vehicle was stopped by a game warden. They hunted southern Potter County, figuring the game wardens there wouldn't know about their history of poaching in Clinton County. However, they never expected that I'd begin looking for them in Potter County. I made a habit of it. They saw me often, and I knew that I was beginning to make life uncomfortable for both of them.

While on night patrol on Christmas Eve 1989, I came upon a pickup truck spotlighting along Dry Run Road in Chapman Township, Clinton County. It was well after legal hours, so I activated my emergency lights and pulled the vehicle over. As I approached the cab, I shined my flashlight in the bed and saw a freshly killed antlerless deer. There was only one person inside, and I ordered him to get out with his hands raised. I shined my flashlight on him with my left hand, while my right hand gripped a holstered .357 magnum revolver. It was Wolfe. I told him to place his hands on the hood of his truck, and then handcuffed him.

"You got me John!" he said. "I never thought you would be out on Christmas Eve."

"Well, you thought wrong." I looked inside the cab of his truck and saw a .30-30 lever action rifle. It was loaded with a single round. I seized the rifle and let Wolfe stand outside while I wrote citations for spotlighting after closing hour, spotlighting while in possession of a firearm, possessing a loaded firearm in a motor vehicle, and killing a deer during closed season. Wolfe pleaded guilty, paid a heavy fine, and had his hunting and trapping privileges revoked for several years.

The following year, on a Friday afternoon in late October, I walked into the Olde Kingsley Inn for a quick bite to eat. This was the former YMCA restaurant and hotel in Renovo that had closed years earlier. Upon entering the dining area, I immediately noticed Coyotee Boy seated at the counter. As he bit into his hamburger, he saw me in the wall mirror in front of him. He put his sandwich down and spun his stool around to face me.

"Sir, can I have a few words with you?" he asked.

I had to look behind me to make sure he wasn't talking to someone else. This wasn't the Coyotee Boy that I knew. His hair was cut short, and he was neatly dressed while wearing a tie. What's more, he addressed me with *sir*, which was not the way Coyotee Boy would normally speak.

"Sure," I said as I walked over and sat down on the stool beside him.

"I quit drinking," he said.

"That's great; glad to hear it," I commented. "So, why are you all dressed up?"

"I just got out of church."

"On Friday?"

"Yessir. Mostly just helping out. They got a big dinner planned for tonight."

"Good for you," I said.

"I quit poaching too."

For a moment, I was speechless. "Well, I'll be straight up front with you Coyotee Boy, all of this is a little hard for me to believe."

"When I was in that Scout rolling down the road, I prayed for the first time in my life," he said. "I promised God I'd change my ways if he spared me. And even though I was being a jerk by shining that spotlight in your face, you tried to save me. So if there is some way that I can help you, I promise that I will."

I couldn't help but think he was playing me for a fool. The man was a career poacher, and he had a mean streak a mile wide. "I appreciate your offer," I said with a tone of skepticism. "But the best way you could help me is by staying out of trouble from now on."

"I intend to do just that," he said. "But I'm serious about my offer to help."

"Help in what way?"

Coyotee Boy looked around the room and then leaned into me. "I know some deer killers worse than me," he whispered. "They're yours if you want them."

I wasn't buying what he had to say, and I didn't want to get chummy with him. "Call if you have something good to tell me." I said. Then I got up and walked out. My number was listed in the phone book, so he was free to contact me with information if he was serious.

A few days later, I received a phone call from Coyotee Boy. He told me he was squirrel hunting with Beefcake Billy, and Billy had killed a doe with his .22 rifle. They had split up, and Coyotee Boy didn't find out about the deer until he returned to Billy's car parked along Barneys Ridge Road south of Renovo. Billy had only removed the hindquarters, and he opened the trunk to show them to Coyotee Boy. The following day Coyotee Boy returned to the area alone and found the remains of the deer.

"I'll take you right to it," He said. It was closed season as well as illegal to use a .22 rifle for big game, so I met Coyotee Boy at the fork of Barneys Ridge Road and Dry Run Road the next morning. We hiked along the edge of a timber clearcut and soon came upon a large white oak tree at the border of the cut area. I could see a deer carcass lying on the ground ahead of us.

I examined the carcass and found that the deer had been shot in the head. I had a small hatchet with me and used it to open the skull where I found a .22 caliber bullet in the brain matter. Unfortunately, it was severely damaged and there wasn't enough remaining for a ballistics examination. My only option was to trick Beefcake Billy into a confession, but I had to make sure he didn't suspect Coyotee Boy was involved.

Still, I had some doubt about Coyotee Boy's story. Why would he turn on a friend? Did Coyotee Boy shoot the deer? Was this a setup? I didn't trust Coyotee Boy any farther than I could throw him. However, I knew that if he had truly changed his ways, he could be a tremendous asset to me as a confidential informant.

I photographed the deer remains and put the bullet in my pocket. While we hiked back to our vehicles, Coyotee Boy talked breathlessly, almost non-stop. He told me he was willing to do whatever was necessary to help me catch some of his friends who were poaching deer. He was clearly excited by the idea that he could play a part in all of this, so I asked him if he was willing to ride along with someone to jacklight a deer while under my strict oversight.

"Yes, I'd love that!" He said. "When can we do it? How about tonight? I can make some phone calls!"

"No, I don't' want to do it like that," I said. "I want you to call me after someone contacts *you* to go with *them*. I don't want you to encourage anyone; it has to be initiated by the other person first."

"Okay, okay…Then what?" he asked eagerly.

"Let's leave it at that for now."

My main concern at the moment was confronting Beefcake Billy about the illegal deer kill without implicating Coyotee Boy. It was all I could think about. After Coyotee Boy got in his truck and drove off, I sat down on a moss-covered log and mentally ran through a bunch of scenarios. It was getting late, and the shadows were getting longer. Soon it was dark, very dark, and this vast remote forest provided an exceptional view of the stars at the edge of the clearcut. But I wasn't ready to go home yet. I gazed upon the starlit sky and prayed for an answer. Moments later, a shooting star blazed across the heavens. *Yes, that's it!* I thought. If I could see a meteor that was sixty or seventy miles away, someone could easily have watched Beefcake Billy from only a few hundred yards.

The following morning I went to Billy's home near Hyner. I rapped on the front door, and a few moments later it slowly opened. Billy looked like he just woke up as he rubbed his eyes and yawned. His upper and lower teeth (incisors) were missing, and all of his molars were gold. He was wearing shorts and a sleeveless T-shirt. He was heavily muscled and bald with a thick beard, reminding me of George "The Animal" Steele, who portrayed a menacing imbecile of 1980s wrestling fame.

"Hi John, what's up?" He asked. Even though I had never met him, most everyone who hunted in this end of the county knew who I was. I had a blank search warrant sticking out of my shirt pocket so it could be readily seen, and I saw him glance briefly at the document.

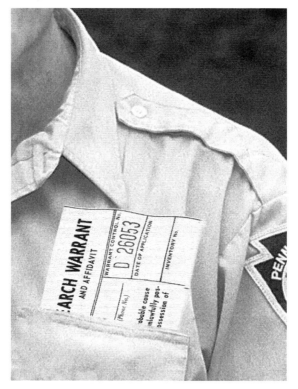

"I want to talk to you about the deer you killed near Barney's Ridge Road the other day," I told him.

"What deer?"

"You know what I'm talking about; let's not play games. An archery hunter watched you shoot it from his treestand on the other side of the clearcut."

"Who?"

"I'm not at liberty to tell you right now."

"Well, I see you have a search warrant."

"Did I say that was for you?"

"No, but you didn't have to. I'm not stupid. You got me." He glanced back inside the house. "Look, my wife is asleep on the couch," he said. "Can I bring the meat outside to you? I don't want you coming into my house if that's okay."

"Sure Billy, that's fine. Just bring it outside and we can get this settled."

"Yes sir," he said. "Just give me a few minutes."

I confiscated the venison and filed citations against Beefcake Billy for killing a deer in closed season and using a .22 caliber rifle to kill big game. Billy pleaded guilty later that week and never suspected that Coyotee Boy was my source.

Days later, when I told Coyotee Boy what happened he became visibly excited. "When can we do this again?" he asked. "I got a lot of friends that want me to hunt deer with them. How about tonight?"

I couldn't help but think this was getting a little weird. It wasn't like I was holding a prison sentence or a huge fine over his head so he'd give up his friends. He actually wanted this, and was getting a thrill out of working with me to catch them!

"I told you before, don't initiate anything," I said. "Call me the next time someone asks you to go with them. It has to be their idea, not yours."

A few weeks later, Coyotee Boy called my home and told me that Willy Nilly and Sammy Sweats asked him to accompany them on a nighttime poaching expedition. That definitely caught my attention, as both of these guys were career poachers, especially crazy Willy Nilly. I told Coyotee Boy that I didn't want him to shoot anything himself. I only wanted him to go along with them, and eventually direct them to where I'd be concealed and watching.

"Tell them you don't feel good," I suggested. "Just lay down in the back seat, tell them you're sick, and don't touch the gun yourself. If they shoot a deer, put a tiny spot of blood on the trunk of the car so I'll know there's a deer inside.

"Okay!" he answered gleefully. "That's perfect! They'll never suspect me."

"Listen to me, and listen good!" I said. "They don't have to shoot anything. There's a heavy fine just for spotlighting a deer with a gun in the car. Tell them you've been watching a big ten-point buck near the Leidy Bridge at Kettle Creek. I'll be hiding nearby. Make sure it's after midnight so it's past quitting time for spotlighting. I'll be able to stop the car for that violation, and when I discover a gun I'll make it look like you're getting arrested too."

"Just be sure to make it look good so they won't suspect me."

"Don't get out of the car when I tell you to," I said. "You might get roughed up a bit, but it'll look real."

Coyotee Boy grinned slyly. "That's pretty shrewd, man. I like it!"

The following night I hid my patrol car near Beaverdam Run along a grassy field bordering Kettle Creek. Ranger was with me, and we waited patiently for the clock to strike twelve. Midnight came and went, and by 2 AM not a single car had passed by.

"Let's go home," Ranger grumbled. "Coyotee Boy is full of it. Nothing is gonna happen tonight!"

"You might be right," I said. "He was supposed to be here by one o'clock. Let's give it another fifteen minutes." I no sooner uttered those words when we heard a vehicle approaching. Moments later, a blue 1980 Chevy drove by with a spotlight shining out the passenger window.

"That's gotta be them!" I said.

Ranger spit a mouthful of tobacco juice out the window and away we went. With tires spinning and my red light and siren blaring, we raced up behind the old Chevy and pulled them over. I focused my emergency spotlight on them, identified myself and used my loud speaker to order them to remain in the car.

Ranger and I approached cautiously while shining our flashlights on the Chevy's rear window and trunk. Bloody handprints were smeared across the entire trunk even though all I asked for was a single spot of blood.

I ordered everyone to exit the car with their hands up. Willy Nilly was the driver, and he got out first. His hands were raised as he turned to face me, but then he grinned at me while lowering his right hand toward his jacket pocket. I grabbed his shoulders, spun him around and slammed him against the side of his car.

"Hands on the roof!" I barked. Willy complied, and I patted him down to check for a weapon. He was clean, so I told him to place his hands behind his back and slapped the handcuffs on him. Meanwhile, Ranger pulled Sammy Sweats from the passenger seat and handcuffed him as well. There was a .22 rifle lying on the floor where Sammy had been sitting.

Coyotee Boy was in the back, and I ordered him to get out of the car. He refused, as we had planned earlier, so I dragged him out, spun him around and slammed him against the trunk. He yelped in pain, and I knew he wasn't acting, but I had to make it look good. I cuffed him and ordered all three men to stand at the side of the road. Then I pulled the keys from the ignition and unlocked the trunk. Two female deer were lying inside, each shot through the head.

I wrote citations for killing two deer in closed season, using an artificial light to hunt deer, and using a .22 rifle to kill big game. The citations for Coyotee Boy were never filed before the district judge, but I gave him copies to make it look like he was fined. Willy Nilly and Sammy Sweats pleaded guilty, paid huge fines, and had their hunting and trapping privileges revoked for several years.

Coyotee Boy was happy with the results. He called me on the phone asking if the fines were paid, and the number of years Willy and Sammy had their licenses revoked. While I appreciated what he did to help me catch these poachers, I had a hard time understanding his glee.

Six weeks later, I received another call from Coyotee Boy. He told me that his brother, Wolfe was hunting while his license was revoked, and that he shot a deer two days before the opening season. He described the location as across from Jews Run, between the railroad tracks and the West Branch of the Susquehanna River. I was shocked by his phone call. In my wildest dreams, I never thought he would turn on his older brother. I knew it would be very difficult for me to interrogate

Wolfe without exposing Coyotee Boy as my informant. I was up half the night thinking about it, and I slowly began putting a plan of action in place. There was a hunting camp across the river within view of where Wolfe shot the deer. If someone was in the camp, they would have been able to see Wolfe hunting, provided they had binoculars or a spotting scope. And because of the distance, there was no way Wolfe could have known whether or not someone was in the camp. I contacted Game Warden Ken Packard who patrolled the southern half of Clinton County and asked him to assist. The following day I called Wolfe on the phone and asked him to meet me at the police station in Renovo.

"Sure John, but why can't we discuss this now?" he asked.

"You'll understand when we meet," I said. "I have something to show you, and it won't take much of your time."

That evening, Wolfe came to the police station as promised. I was sitting behind a desk with a large 80 mm tripod-mounted scope just off to my left. I had placed an empty chair in front of my desk, and Game Warden Packard was dressed in full camouflage clothing while leaning against a wall to my right. I knew Wolfe didn't know Ken, who would play an important role in my attempt to get Wolfe to admit he killed the deer.

Wolfe was a few minutes early and visibly nervous when he walked into the police station. He glanced over at Ken who stared back at him without saying a word. Wolfe looked at the scope while only briefly making eye contact with me. He was five-foot-ten with a heavy beard and dark brown hair that fell to his shoulders. His eyes were black with thick eyebrows that grew together.

"Sit Wolfe," I said firmly while pointing to the chair in front of me.

"Hi John, what's this all about?" he asked while taking a seat.

I looked over at Ken Packard. "Is this him?"

Ken nodded affirmatively while continuing to stare at Wolfe.

"Thank you sir," I said. "Have a nice evening."

Game Warden Packard walked out of the building, and Wolfe started to sweat.

"Wolfe, do you know what this is?" I asked, pointing at the spotting scope.

"Yes, that's one heck of a scope you got there!"

"Well it's not mine; it belongs to Sergeant Ken, the man who just left."

"Sergeant?"

"Yes, he's a state trooper who was staying at a camp along the riverbank at Jews Run yesterday. He was scoping a big doe across the river near the railroad tracks when he heard a shot and it dropped."

Wolfe looked down at the floor and slowly shook his head. I was certain he knew about the camp; it could easily be seen from where he was hunting. "He got a good look at you while using this spotting scope," I continued. "And he just positively identified you. What do you have to say for yourself?"

Wolfe blew a long sigh and shrugged. "When you're caught, you're caught," he said. "I did it; I won't fight it in court and I'll pay the fine. Just do me one small favor."

"Depends," I answered. "What's the favor?"

"Don't let Coyotee Boy find out about this; my little brother looks up to me, I wouldn't want him to know I got caught."

With that remark, I had to break eye contact for a moment as I wondered what kind of warped mindset Coyotee Boy possessed. Wolfe deserved a big fine along with several years added to his license revocation, but his request was a bit hard for me to deal with. Wolfe was a dyed-in-the-wool poacher, but I never considered him a threat. Unlike his brother, Wolfe was always friendly, even though we were adversaries.

"Why would I say anything to Coyotee Boy?"

"Right, you wouldn't. But I was hoping you wouldn't say anything to anybody at all. Maybe keep it a secret between us. I guess it was a dumb request."

"I'll do my best," I said. But he knew the word would probably get out. That's what happens in small towns across America, and Renovo was no exception. Wolfe wouldn't be able to hunt legally for the next seven years, and I figured it was only a matter of time before our paths would cross again.

Several weeks went by and I received another phone call from Coyotee Boy. Danny Dred, a well-known poacher, wanted some help to jacklight a deer. It was closed season, and I had been after Danny for many years. I told Coyotee Boy to bring him to Crawford Hollow Road at the head of Cooks Run. It was a dead-end road, and a great location to set up a decoy, as I didn't want them to shoot a live deer.

"Tell him you've been seeing a lot of deer along Crawford Hollow Road," I said. "I'll have a decoy deer set up. You won't be able to miss it with a spotlight."

"Okay, will do!" Coyotee Boy said cheerily. A chill ran down my spine knowing that Danny was his lifelong best friend.

I contacted Game Warden Ken Packard for assistance, and he was more than happy to help. Ken is among the cream of the crop for state game wardens in Pennsylvania, and if he set his mind to catch someone, it was only a matter of time until it happened.

Ken and I put the decoy deer along Crawford Hollow Road where we believed it couldn't be missed. The eyes would glow when a spotlight hit it. It was perfect! Coyotee Boy was instructed to come by with Danny between midnight and one AM, so Ken and I got into position early and waited. We were in the middle of nowhere; the only sound we heard was a pair of barred owls calling to each other, and we didn't expect to see anyone other than Coyotee Boy and Danny Dred that night.

By one o'clock, Ken was getting anxious. We had been sitting in my patrol car for three hours without seeing another vehicle.

"Maybe we should go look for them," Ken said while faking a yawn to punctuate his boredom.

"Okay, I get it." I said with a chuckle. "But I think we should stay put. Coyotee Boy has never failed to deliver;

they'll be here; I'm sure of it." Although I was confident they'd show up, it was unlike Coyotee Boy to be this late. After another thirty minutes passed, Ken started getting impatient again.

"Come on John, let's go find them," he pressed.

"Hang in there Ken," I said. "Let's give it another half hour. If they don't show up by then, we'll go looking for them."

Ken glanced at his wristwatch. "Fair enough, John. Thirty minutes and counting."

Moments later, we could hear the distant rumble of an approaching vehicle followed by the glow of its headlights.

"That's gotta be them," I said as the rays of a spotlight beamed across the sky. Soon they were directly across from the decoy. We sat in complete silence, expecting them to light up the decoy within seconds, but the Chevy pickup rumbled right on by without even noticing it.

"I can't believe it!" exclaimed Ken. "How could they miss seeing the deer?"

"I don't know," I said. "Let's just sit tight; they have to go by again on the way out."

Suddenly we heard two shots! Both of them came from the truck's position below us. It was a dead-end road, so we waited for them to come back out, but Ken soon became anxious. He got out of the car and walked over to the road to watch and listen while pacing back and forth. His persona reminded me of a Belgian Malinois, a high-strung dog breed used by police and military around the world. Ken was always restless, wanting to charge after the bad guy instantly, and there was no such thing as failure in his mindset.

A half hour went by when Ken heard Danny's truck approaching and jumped back inside my patrol car. As soon as they passed our position, I turned on the emergency lights and ripped out of our hiding spot onto the road behind them. Danny's truck sped up and started to pull away but the old Chevy was no match for my patrol car, and he soon stopped in the middle of the road ahead of us.

I stopped behind them with my high beams shining on the truck and we got out and approached on each side of the vehicle with our flashlights illuminating the interior.

"State game wardens!" I called. "Get out of the truck with your hands in the air."

Danny Dred exited the driver's side and Coyotee Boy got out of the passenger side, both with their hands held high. I ordered them to put their hands on the roof of the pickup, and as we approached closer I could see two dead deer in the bed. We patted them down for weapons and handcuffed them behind their backs. I watched the men closely while Ken searched the truck. Then, when he pulled a loaded Remington .243 rifle from floor of the cab, Coyotee Boy started shouting obscenities at us. It was a smart move on his part, and a tip-off that he was worried Danny suspected it was a setup.

Ken looked at me with grave concern, and I knew he was thinking the same thing. Danny had a long criminal record including aggravated assault, and Coyotee Boy's days would be numbered if he thought he was involved.

Coyote Boy continued to scream all kinds of cuss words at us. It was his way of begging me to come to his rescue. He was scared. Real scared.

Danny was watching close, waiting to see what I'd do, so I walked up to Coyotee Boy and slapped him across the face so hard he fell to the ground. Then I grabbed him and pulled him to his feet.

"I'm gonna report you!" Coyotee Boy said with a whimper.

I looked over at Ken. "Did you see anything?"

"Yeah. I saw Coyotee Boy trip and fall on his face."

Next I turned to Danny. "How about you? See anything?"

He studied me carefully for a moment, then spat on the ground and looked away.

I looked back at Coyotee Boy and he winked at me as blood trickled from the corner of his mouth.

This is getting crazy, I thought. It had to end after tonight. There are few secrets in small towns, and Coyotee Boy was finished as far as I was concerned. One more arrest involving him with a friend would be too great a risk to his safety.

A few days later, I met Coyotee Boy at a remote location and told him we were finished. I thanked him for helping me catch poachers who I had been after for many years.

"I couldn't have done it without your help," I told him.

He looked straight at me, speechless at first, and I could see a tear forming in his eye. He started to say something, his mouth trembled a bit, and then he bowed his head.

"I ain't a boy; I'm a man," he muttered bitterly.

"Yes, of course you are," I said. "This isn't about…"

"*Stop!*" he shrieked, looking up at me. "I don't want to hear no more from you!"

He walked over to his truck a few yards away and stood silently by the door for a moment. Then he turned to face me uttering a series of short howls that would rise and fall in pitch, interrupted by a chorus of yips, yaps, and barks. It was a perfect imitation of a mated pair of coyotes, with the male howling while the female offers her yips, barks, and brief howls. I was shocked by his ability to imitate the sounds to a degree that seemed wildly inhuman.

When he finally stopped, the expression of sadness he had moments ago became fiercely hostile. He stared menacingly at me while his hands clenched into tight fists.

I took a step forward and palmed the pepper spray canister on my duty belt. Coyotee Boy instantly recognized my change of position and stepped back. His fists opened, and a sinister grin formed across his lips.

"The game is on!" he cried gleefully. "The real Coyotee Boy is back, and the deer are gonna drop like flies!"

Coyotee Boy jumped inside his truck, slammed the door shut, and shouted, "You'll never catch me again!" Then he quickly sped onto the highway toward Renovo.

I should have slapped him a lot harder! I thought.

I knew Coyotee Boy was serious, and he would be poaching a lot of deer. I was spread thin with a 450 square mile patrol district and only one deputy. The odds were clearly in his favor, and he was known for thrill kills, just dropping them where they stood and driving away.

I drove home feeling a bit depressed knowing I was played by Coyotee Boy. Even if I caught him poaching again, he'd never quit. I walked inside, sat down at my desk and thought long and hard about how to stop the impending slaughter of perhaps hundreds of deer. Hours passed before it came to me, and I reached for the phone and dialed.

"Hello?" returned a familiar voice on the other end.

"Hey Big, it's John. I have a favor to ask..."

The thin mask of civilization is delicate and easily cast aside. What lies behind is savage and unforgiving.

Acknowledgments

I thank my beautiful wife Denise for her encouragement and help in bringing my first book to fruition. She was always willing to review my writing, and provide meaningful suggestions to enhance each chapter.

Thanks to my twin brother, Bill for his advice, and for spending many hours reviewing, revising, and publishing this book.

Thanks to the deputy game wardens that served with me during my long career, most of whom were represented by the character "Ranger" in this book.

John "Pete" Rathmell

David Snodgrass

Jude Richardson

Tom Schmoke

Jim Tolomay

Joe Brookens